NO PLACE TO HIDE

NO PLACE TO HIDE

A COMPANY AT NUI BA DEN

BILL SLY

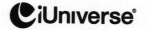

NO PLACE TO HIDE
A COMPANY AT NUI BA DEN

iUniverse books may be ordered through booksellers or by contacting:

iUniverse
1663 Liberty Drive
Bloomington, IN 47403
www.iuniverse.com
1-800-Authors (1-800-288-4677)

Because of the dynamic nature of the Internet, any web addresses or links contained in this book may have changed since publication and may no longer be valid. The views expressed in this work are solely those of the author and do not necessarily reflect the views of the publisher, and the publisher hereby disclaims any responsibility for them.

Any people depicted in stock imagery provided by Thinkstock are models, and such images are being used for illustrative purposes only. Certain stock imagery © Thinkstock.

ISBN: 978-1-5320-0304-2 (sc)
ISBN: 978-1-5320-0305-9 (e)

Library of Congress Control Number: 2016913599

Print information available on the last page.

iUniverse rev. date: 08/24/2016

This book is dedicated to the memory of these brave soldiers who gave their all to protect their fellow soldiers and to those who were wounded. It is also to the men whose injuries are on the inside and those who will never forget what happened to them in these two days.

Second Infantry (Mech) Second Infantry, First Infantry Division

Alpha Company as their names appear on the Vietnam Memorial:
- Richard L. Buckles Pacific Grove, California
- Steven T. Cummins Eau Gallie, Florida
- Richard A. England Girard, Illinois
- Calvin Harris Rosedale, Louisiana
- George S. Kimmel Cumberland, Maryland
- Johnny L. King Sanford, North Carolina
- Calvin G. Maguire Altonna, Pennsylvania
- Robert J. Sires Spring Grove, Minnesota
- Daniel L. Wagenaar Richland, Washington

Charlie Company as their names appear on the Vietnam Memorial:
- Steven W. Bradbury Wichita, Kansas
- Robert E. Worrell Portsmouth, Virginia

To the living we owe respect,
But to the dead we owe only the
Truth.
—Voltaire

Contents

Acknowledgments

I would first of all like to thank the soldiers with whom I have corresponded for the last twenty years. They have really told this story; I just put their thoughts in a timeline. I would like to thank Joe Ladensack. He has acted as my adviser all these years and recently has contributed some chapters of his own. His wonderful wife, Anita, has been with us for the entire rewrite and has been a great help to us. I would like to thank my son, Bob, who helped me write the book when I was emotionally wrung out and needed his help. His darling wife, Lisa, helped set up cloud collaboration and tutored us on its use. My daughter, Melissa Brito, has always been my number one supporter, and she was especially helpful in the writing of the introduction. Her husband, Jeff, set up the pictures in the book, and I thank them both. There is a special group that I would like to thank—the staff of the First Infantry Division Museum. The museum director, Paul Herbert, and the director, Gayln Piper, spent many long hours improving my original work. Director Eric Gillespie and Historian Andrew Woods taught me how to find the awards for the soldiers in this battle. Without those, the book would have been much tougher to write.

About the Author

Some men were drafted into the army; some volunteered; and I, Bill Sly, was kidnapped by our government. When I entered the university, I was declared unfit for Reserve Officers' Training Corps because I had a ruptured eardrum. But during my senior year in college, I received a letter from my draft board that said essentially, "According to our records you will be graduating from the University of South Dakota on June 1, 1968. Your S-1 (Student) deferment runs out as of that date. We are requesting that you report to the Sioux Falls Induction station on June 4, 1968, to take a physical so that your draft status can be updated."

After that physical, all fifty of us who had reported there were told that we had passed. I noticed a soldier locking the front door so that no one could escape. We were then told to stand and heard, "Repeat after me. 'I—state your name …'" We were not allowed to phone home to tell anyone the news. We were put on a bus out the back door and then loaded into an airplane. Our tickets showed that we were to change planes at the Denver airport. It was from there that I was able to call home and to my fiancée to tell everyone that I was on my way to Fort Lewis, Washington, to begin my basic training.

After training and a thirty-day R&R, I was sent to Vietnam as an 11-Bravo, combat infantryman. I was sent out to join Bravo Company 2/2 (Mech) First Infantry Division to begin my real education on war. I didn't know it then, but a man who knew me at USD saw me go through the battalion and put my name as his replacement in the S-1, Awards and Decorations Department.

While working there, I had the pleasure and honor of writing some very important awards. S. Sgt. James Bondsteel received the Medal of Honor that I wrote. I also wrote up the battalion for a unit citation that was approved as a Valorous Unit Award.

During this time, I endured some things that were very hard on me. The first was when I learned that my best friend in the field had been killed one night while on ambush. I took the news very hard, and I believed at the time (and still do) that the whole damn country of Vietnam wasn't worth the life of "Tiny."

Tiny was the squad's M-60 gunner, and I was his assistant gunner, meaning that we lived closer together than many married couples. My job was to always be within fifteen feet of Tiny and to provide additional ammunition when he needed it. I will never get over his death or the guilt that comes with knowing that I was safely in the rear while the man who had counted on me for two months bled to death.

After my R&R in Hawaii with my fiancée, I was met at the helipad in Dau Tieng and told to change clothes and report back to take the next helicopter to a battle at the base of Nui Ba Den. This is the story of that battle.

I left Vietnam and the army on January 6, 1970. I turned twenty-four that day, and it was the happiest day of my life. I was going to put an end to my war and never look back. After spending some time with my family, I went to O'Hare to meet my fiancée, but when we met up, I heard the greeting many other returning vets got—"Bill, I've decided that you don't fit in with my new friends, so I have decided that I never want to see you again. Good-bye."

This allowed me to meet a different woman who did not know me before Vietnam, and I was able to put it behind me completely. We began our marriage by moving around the United States, living in seven different states in the first seven years of our marriage. At that time, I didn't realize that I was exhibiting classic symptoms of PTSD. I got around for about fifteen years, and then I began having dreams and flashbacks about my time in Vietnam.

My career suffered, and my marriage became rocky. I decided that since I had a degree in education, I would make a career change and become a teacher. However, the State of Illinois would not certify me until I had taken an additional course and completed a series of tests.

This gave me some time to begin working on this story. I went to the First Infantry Division Museum and found out that all the awards that had been issued to First Division soldiers were on file there. I began to read them and record those that interested me. In order to do this, I had to review ten thousand awards that were earned during the second half of 1969. I found that the nightmares and flashbacks became overwhelming unless I found only a few names at a time and then gave my mind a rest.

By the time I had collected most of the names, two events had happened that ultimately helped me complete this story—my wife divorced me, and my dad died. In the divorce, we sold our house and paid off all our debts. My mother had died in 1987, so when my father died, I was the appointed executor of the will. As a result, I had some time on my hands, and I was being paid to be the executor of the estate. I found a list of many of Alpha Company's soldiers with background information, and I sent letters to some of them.

I was not sure what kind of reception my letter would get. After twenty-five years, many men might just want to forget the whole thing. To my relief, men thanked me for finally telling this story.

What follows is the story, as told to me and by the men who lived through those days.[58]

Glossary of Terms

I realize that the glossary is usually placed at the end of the publication. However, this book is filled with many words, phrases, and abbreviations that make little sense if you do not have a military background. It is suggested that you review these terms and their meanings before you begin the text.

US Army Ranks

Enlisted

Pay Grade	Abbrevation	Rank
E-1	Pvt	Private
E-2	Pvt	Private
E-3	Pfc	Private First Class
E-4	Cpl	Corporal
E-4	SP4	Specialist Fourth Class
E-5	SP5	Specialist Fifth Class

Noncommissioned Officers (NCO)

Pay Grade	Abbreviation	Rank
E-5	Sgt	Sergeant
E-6	S. Sgt	Staff Sergeant
E-7	Sgt FC	Sergeant First Class
E-8	MSG	Master Sergeant
E-8	1st Sgt	First Sergeant
E-9	SM	Sergeant Major
E-9	CSM	Command Sergeant Major

Pay Grade	Warrant Officer* Abbreviation	Rank
W-1	WO	Warrant Officer
W-2	CWO	Chief Warrant Officer
W-3	CWO	Chief Warrant Officer
W-4	CWO	Chief Warrant Officer

*A warrant officer is normally a highly skilled, single-track specialist. Examples are aviation (pilots), maintenance, and food specialists. They are specialists unlike commissioned officers, who are generalists. The purpose of the army warrant officer is to serve in specific areas that require greater expertise, longevity, and management skills. W-1 is addressed as "Mr." W2–4 are addressed as "Chief." A warrant officer outranks all noncommissioned officers and is below the rank of second lieutenant.

Pay Grade	Officers Abbreviation	Rank
0-1	2nd Lt.	Second Lieutenant
0-2	1st Lt.	First Lieutenant
0-3	Capt.	Captain
0-4	Maj.	Major
0-5	Lt. Col.	Lieutenant Colonel
0-6	Col.	Colonel
0-7	Brig. Gen.	Brigadier General
0-8	Maj. Gen.	Major General
0-9	Lt. Gen.	Lieutenant General
0-10	Gen.	General

Chain of Command

Organization	Authorized Strength	Rank
Battalion Commander	920	Lieutenant Colonel
Company Commander	170	Captain
Platoon Leader	44	1st or 2nd Lt
Platoon Sergeant	44	Sergeant First Class
Squad Leader	11	Staff Sergeant
Fire Team Leader	5	Sergeant

In case a leader is unable to perform his or her command, such as in the case that he or she is killed or wounded, the person in the next-lower rank moves up and takes command.

In this battle, the company commander position shifted from Capt. Buckles to a first lieutenant (Williams), to another first lieutenant (Mulhern), and then to a second lieutenant (Ladensack). All sergeants above E-5 were killed or evacuated, raising the possibility that a sergeant (Wullenweber) may have become the company commander if Ladensack and Mathews were KIA or WIA. This progression did take place at times in Vietnam.[1]

Terms

105 mm howitzer	Artillery weapon with 105-milli-meter-diameter bore that can be towed or airlifted, with a range of 7.1 miles and a shell weight of forty-two pounds
155 mm howitzer	Artillery weapon with 155-milli-meter-diameter bore that can be towed or airlifted, with a range of

	nine miles and a shell weight of ninety pounds; one version can be fully tracked and self-propelled
First Infantry Division	"Big Red One," the eighteen-thousand-soldier division to which the 2/2 Mech was assigned
2/6	Radio call sign of the platoon leader (6) of the Second Platoon (2) on the company net
Twenty-Fifth Infantry Division	"Tropic Lighting," the division that controlled the 2/2 during the battle of July 12–13, 1969
45	A .45-caliber pistol carried by some army personnel
.50 gunner	Member of the APC crew who fired the .50-caliber machine gun
8" gun	Large howitzer with an eight-inch bore, a range of 15.5 miles, and a shell weight of two hundred pounds
81 mm mortar	High-angle artillery weapon that is carried by a mortar platoon APC; there are three such APCs per mortar platoon
90 mm HE rounds	High-explosive rounds fired from the main gun of the M48A-3 tank
ACAV	Armored Calvary Assault Vehicle, APC modified with extra machine guns and gun shields
ADC	Assistant division commander, usually a brigadier general
AK-47	Standard military semi or fully automatic assault rifle in communist countries

Alpha	One of the five companies in a battalion, made up of 170–180 men
Alpha 2/34	A tank company from the Twenty-Fifth Infantry Division that was under the control of the 2/2 (Mech)
ACM with V	Army Commendation Medal for Valor, fifth-highest medal for valor
APC	Armored Personnel Carrier (A113A), a thirteen-ton tracked vehicle that usually had a .50 gunner, a driver, a track commander, a 60 machine gunner, an assistant 60 gunner, an M-79 gunner, and some infantrymen carrying M-16s. A platoon consisted of four APCs.
ARC Light	Code name for a B-52 bombing strike using 500-pound and 750-pound bombs covering an area three thousand meters long and three hundred meters wide
B-52 bomb crater	Hole in the ground left after a large bomb explodes from a B-52 strike, often thirty meters wide and ten meters deep
Battalion (BN)	Military unit consisting of five companies—A, B, C, D and HHC—of approximately 920 men and 70 armored vehicles. The actual number of men in the field was normally below 750.
BDA	Bomb Damage Assessment, conducted by looking at photos or physically observing damage caused by bombs

Berm	Raised area of dirt used for defensive purposes
Black Virgin Mountain	Mountain near Tay Ninh in the Twenty-Fifth Division zone that was formed by two extinct volcanoes, honeycombed with caves and tunnels; also called Nui Ba Den
Booby traps	Any device that will harm a person who steps on it or causes it to explode, like a mine
Bronze Star with V	Fourth-highest valor award
CO	Two meanings—either commanding officer or conscientious objector
Concertina wire	Rolls of barbed wire used for defensive purposes
Charlie	One of the five companies in a battalion
Cu Chi	Headquarters of the Twenty-Fifth Infantry Division fifteen miles north west of Saigon
Claymore mine	US-made device that was placed on the ground and fired electronically; it consists of an explosive device and hundreds of ball bearings
Conscientious objector	A person who either refuses to serve in the military for religious or moral reasons or who refuses to carry a weapon; many conscientious objectors served as medics
Coordinates	Six numbers on a map—two sets of three—to locate the positions to drop bombs, mortars, and artillery
CSM	Command Sergeant Major—highest-ranking noncommissioned officer in the battalion

Curtain of steel	Defensive strategy to fill the area between the US forces and the enemy with explosives, such as mortars, bombs, and artillery
Dau Tieng	Base camp northwest of Saigon near the Cambodian border that was used at various times by the First Infantry Division and the Twenty-Fifth Infantry Division, located near the Michelin Rubber Plantation
Dismounted operation	Infantry performing a mission apart from their APCs, something seldom done in a mechanized unit except for small ambushes
Dustoff	Helicopter medical evacuation mission
Elephant grass	Grass that grows in the tropics six to seven feet tall with edges that will cut your hand if you try to move it
FO	Forward observer, member of an artillery unit attached to an infantry unit for the purpose of calling in and directing artillery, helicopter gunships, and air strikes
Fire support base	Permanent defensive position, normally containing artillery battery (6) guns and defended by one infantry company
Four deuce mortars	Large mortars with 4.2-inch-diameter bores
Flying crane	Heavy-lift helicopter that resembles a praying mantis, such as the Sikorsky S-64 Skycrane, with a payload of 29,000 pounds

Fougasse	Container (usually a fifty-five-gallon drum) filled with napalm and placed in the ground with explosives underneath, used for defense
Hunter-killer team	One OH-6A scout helicopter and one AH-1G Cobra gunship
Huey	UH-1 utility helicopter called various names depending on its use: Slick for cargo or troop carrier; Command and Control (C&C) for high-ranking commanders; and Log Bird if hauling supplies, food, or mail
Hull defilade	Part of a defensive structure that allows a tank or track to get into a hole so that the hull can avoid being hit by an RPG but still use its main guns
Jungle busting	Operation in which tanks and APCs act like bulldozers in clearing jungle; it's hard on vehicles and soldiers with minimal results
KIA	Killed in action
Klick	One kilometer or one thousand meters, a standard unit of measure in the US Army
Landing zone (LZ)	Area cleared to land helicopters
LAW	The M72 LAW (light antitank weapon) is a light, portable, one-shot, 66 millimeter, unguided antitank weapon that is also used against fighting positions
Leg Company	Designation that mechanized infantry gave to the infantry that had to walk to the battle; they referred to themselves as grunts.

LOH	Light observation helicopter; pronounced "loach"; either a Hughes OH-6A Cayuse or Bell OH-58A Kiowa
M-16	Standard US Army rifle, semi or fully automatic with twenty- or thirty-round magazines
M-60	US-made 7.62-millimeter machine gun that could be mounted and fired from an APC or taken off for dismounted operations
M-79	Thumper, single-shot, shoulder-fired grenade launcher that can fire a variety of grenades, high explosives, smoke, illumination, etc.
Mad Minute	Defensive strategy in which everyone on the perimeter fires his weapon on full automatic for twenty seconds to a minute; used to provoke an enemy attack
Mech	Abbreviation for "mechanized," used to describe a unit in which infantrymen are carried by and supported by armored vehicles
Medevac zone	Area near a battle zone from which wounded are evacuated, especially by helicopter
MIA	Missing in action
Nui Ba Den	Vietnamese name for a mountain northwest of Saigon that Americans called the Black Virgin Mountain
Nui Cao	Smaller mountain west of Nui Ba Den, called Little Sister by the Americans

NVA	North Vietnamese Army
Op-con	Operational control; term for a unit's borrowing part of another unit
Phantom	F-4, main US fighter bomber
Platoon leader	Usually a lieutenant, but anyone who is the ranking member of a platoon and is in command of the unit, normally composed of forty men
Platoon sergeant	Ranking noncommissioned officer in a platoon, usually a SFC (Sergeant First Class)
Point	First person walking or armored vehicle in a group
Poncho liner	Soft liner of a raincoat used by soldiers as a blanket
Popped a bush	Fired on an enemy force while on ambush patrol
Punji stake	Bamboo stake placed in a camouflaged hole and often covered with human feces to promote infection
Radio net	All radios being set at the same frequency. The military radio can change frequencies, so all commanders in a company set their radios on the same frequency and that became the company net. All company commanders set a second radio on the battalion frequency, and that became the battalion net.
Ramps	Backs of APCs (M113) that were raised or lowered from inside the vehicles

Recon platoon leader	Usually a senior first lieutenant but anyone who is the ranking member of a platoon and is in command of the unit, normally composed of seventy men
RIF	Reconnaissance in Force, words used by the US Army after "search and destroy" became politically incorrect
RON	Remain Overnight or Rest Overnight, words used to designate a company's night defensive position, any place a company spent the night in a defensive formation
RPD	Communist-made light machine gun that used standard AK-47 ammunition (7.62 mm) but was belt fed and had a slower rate of fire than the AK-47
RPG	Rocket-propelled grenade, a communist-made, shoulder-fired grenade launcher used to put holes in APCs and tanks with the expectation that ammunition and fuel would explode inside and destroy the vehicle. The RPG has a shaped charge and must strike the vehicle at a ninety-degree angle for maximum efficiency.
RPG screen	Chain-link fence installed at least six inches away from the hull of an APC or tank so that the RPG explodes harmlessly against the screen and leaves the APC intact

RTO	Radio telephone operator, the soldier carrying a radio and assigned to follow an officer to convey his communications
S-3	Battalion operations officer, usually a major; in this battle, it was Major George Forrest
Silver Star	Third-highest valor award
SitRep	Situation report given orally at battalion, below which were included the results of combat, WIA, KIA, and other information
SOP	Standard Operating Procedures, the prescribed method for executing a task
Tank	M48A-3 Patton Tank, a diesel tank with one 90 millimeter main gun, one .50-caliber machine gun, and one M-60 machine gun
Tay Ninh	City northwest of Saigon, four klicks from Nui Ba Den
TOC	Tactical Operations Center, where commander and his staff conduct planning, briefing, and other command activities. When located at a fire support base, it is housed in a large bunker. In the field, it is called a jump TOC and is housed in several modified APCs (M-577).
Top	Highest-ranking noncommissioned officer in a company or battalion
Track	Slang for an APC, Armored Personnel Carrier, M113A-1,with a diesel engine that carried a crew of

	one driver, one .50-caliber machine gun gunner, and an eight- to twelve-man infantry squad
Valorous Unit Award	Award given to a unit as opposed to an individual, equal to a Silver Star
WIA	Wounded in action
XO	Executive Officer, the second-highest ranking office in a unit; usually a major in a battalion or a first lieutenant in a company who assumes his commander's duties in his absence

Glossary of Nicknames

2/6	2nd Lt. Joseph Ladensack, Second Platoon A
Chief	Chief SP4 Jimmy Begay, Third Platoon A
Doc D	SP5 Elmer Dehaven, Company Medic A
Firefight	1st Lt. Williams, Third Platoon A
FO	Forward Observer, First Lieutenant Toney Mathews Co A1/5
Hippie	SP4 Ray Courson, .50 gunner of Medic APC A
Old Man	Capt. Richard Buckles A
Popcorn	SP4 David Anderson, Third Platoon A
Ram-Jet	SP4 Roger Hulsey, First Platoon A
Rocky	SP4 John Rockafellow III, Third Platoon A
Spike	SP4 Donovan Kolness, First Platoon A
Tennessee	A soldier who doesn't want his name in this book A
Top	1st Sgt. Jimmy Thomas A
Van	Van Morrison, Driver of Medic APC A

Wully	Sgt. Gary Wullenweber, Second Platoon A
XO	Executive Officer Hugh Evans A
Bob	PFC Robert Streightiff C
Doc Baehr	SP5 Fred Baehr C 2/2 Medic C
Jim	1st Lt. James Brezovec C
Banks	SP4 Chip Banks A
Jerry	Sgt. Jerry Campbell A
Phil	S. Sgt. Phil Deering A
Capt. Howard	Capt. Carrol Howard C
Bill	SP4 Bill Sly HHC
Lt. Col. Vinson	Lt. Col. Newell Vinson HHC
Forrest	Maj. George Forrest HHC
Combs	Capt. Dudley (Pete) Combs 1st Infantry Division
Al	SP4 Alvin Howard A
Pat	Second Lt. Pat McCoy B 1/2
Lugo	Second Lt. Sergio Lugo C
Kimmell	Private First Class George Kimmell A
Mulhern	1st Lt. Mike Mulhern A
Heick	SP4 James (Jack) Heick C
Squirrel	SP4 Robert Worrell A
Miranda	SP5 Mike Miranda A
Lee	SP4 Lee Stember C
Gilliam	SP4 Maurice Gilliam A
Sammy	SP4 Sammy La Bastida A
Tony	Sgt. Tony Lambardi C
Don	SP4 Don Coughennower C
Leo	SP4 Leo Schlotterer C
Hale	SP4 Jim Hale A

ACC	Alpha Company Clerk A
Mathews	1st Lt. Toney Mathews E 1/5 Artillery
Porky	SP4 Bob Douglas A

Prologue

The swirling helicopter blades slowed as the unit historian ducked and ran to meet the battalion commander. It was the evening of July 12, 1969, just at the base of the mountain called Nui Ba Den. After the obligatory salutes were exchanged, the lieutenant colonel motioned me (Second Lt. Joe Ladensack) forward because I was the lone surviving company officer from the battle that had ended a couple of hours earlier. Lt. Col. Vinson introduced the soldier in a fresh uniform and a combat infantryman badge to me. I was covered with mud and blood from my men's and my own wounds, and my shirt had been ripped to make bandages. We followed the lieutenant colonel in side. I found out that he was SP4 Bill Sly and that he had recently graduated from the University of South Dakota. He entered college with a ruptured eardrum and was declared unfit for ROTC. He was drafted just four days after graduating, his eardrum now intact, and sent to Vietnam as an infantryman. After some time in the field as an infantryman, he was selected to become the unit historian.[7]

At the meeting, Bill was ordered to immediately write citations for medals that would be given to the battle's survivors. Within five days, the division commander would pin Purple Hearts, Silver Stars, Bronze Stars, and Army commendations medals on the chests of the beleaguered soldiers. My immediate concern was to reconsolidate the company; prepare the men for their next mission, which

I was told would come very soon; and contact the first sergeant (1st Sgt. Jimmy Thomas) and the company clerk (Sgt. Charles Flickner) as we began to account for the dead, wounded, and survivors.

I told Bill, "Here's how it started. Last night we were treated to an awesome display of raw power. Two groups of B-52 bombers had rained havoc on the mountain. I woke up this morning as a second lieutenant in charge of a platoon. Throughout the day, every officer above me except the FO has been killed or wounded. When you write the awards, I want you to remember that because, for many reasons, this battle is not like many others. We were moving in a military manner right up to the point that we got on the berm at the bottom of the hill. Two things happened. First, there were only a few ways up the mountain. This meant that a number of people had to take an existing route that was completely visually blocked. When we got to a place to move either left or right, there was no way to know which of the choices was best. We ran into people from different platoons and squads. Second, as Americans, we led from the front. This means that as soon as we entered the maze of huge rocks, we lost sight of all of the people for which we were responsible. We could not see forward or sideways. We could see only the people beneath us who had not yet begun to climb. We were blind, and from that moment, it was each soldier making decisions of his own."[7]

Let's start at the beginning."

Chapter 1: Actions around An Loc

2/2 (Mech) May 22, 1969–July 10, 1969

May 23, 1969

For the three days of May 23, 24, and 25, 1969, the 2/2 (Mech) was engaged in a huge battle with the North Vietnamese Army (NVA) at An Loc, a town sixty miles north of Saigon. After the final day, the 2/2 (Mech) had killed an estimated 350 North Vietnamese and had destroyed the fighting effectiveness of the entire North Vietnamese 141st Regiment. The battle resulted in numerous awards for the men and the battalion, including a Valorous Unit Citation for the battalion, a Medal of Honor for S. Sgt. James Bondsteel, two Distinguished Service Crosses, fourteen Silver Stars, numerous Bronze Stars, and an ACM with V. This action was part of an overall successful operation stopping an NVA offensive involving two divisions whose mission was to cut off forward elements of allied forces around Tay Ninh, Dau Tieng, An Loc, and Quan Loi.[5]

In early June of 1969, the men of the 2/2 (Mech) participated in a four-day battle against North Vietnamese regulars and again defeated them soundly, leaving 160 dead North Vietnamese in the field.[5]

The men of the battalion had come to look upon themselves as pretty bad characters who could and did beat the NVA and the Viet Cong (VC) at every turn. These battles caused a number of casualties, and many of the men who were decorated were also wounded. However, due to the tremendous turnover in personnel, by the time the battalion got to the Black Virgin, only four of the men who had won the Silver Stars were still with Alpha.

On June 23, 1969, the battalion moved to Dau Tieng (see map), a base camp in the Tay Ninh province, along with the rest of the First Brigade of the First Infantry Division. During the evenings, the NVA would rocket and mortar the compound.[7]

The battalion was commanded by Lt. Col. Newell E. Vinson, who was born in Pennsylvania to a Navy family but grew up in California and on the East Coast. He called Alexandria, Virginia, home. He had been instructing social studies classes at West Point prior to coming to Vietnam. He had been scheduled to take over the battalion on the sixth of June, but the battalion was then in a battle and the ceremony didn't take place until three days later.[5]

The battalion command sergeant major was James E Knox. The forty-five-year-old Knox was an extremely able soldier and NCO. We felt we were very lucky to have him as our go-to guy. 2/6 remembers Command Sgt. Maj. Knox in this way: "It is often a truism to say that someone is a 'soldier's soldier,' but this is the least I could say about Command Sgt. Maj. Knox. He was a veteran of WWII and Korea and was on his second tour of Vietnam. With the scar that ran down his cheek to the corner of his mouth, he looked like he may have also been one of the three hundred Spartans at Thermopylae." 2/6 remembers that Command Sgt. Maj. Knox loved his soldiers and took great care of them. He would also often counsel junior officers if they requested him to do so. Joe states, "In 1979 Mike Mulhern and I attended a First Infantry Division reunion at Fort Riley. As soon as we arrived at the reception, Command Sgt. Maj. Knox recognized us and briskly walked over and carried on a long conversation about our serving together. It meant a lot to the both of us. He was a class act."[7]

On June 26, Lt. Col. Vinson sent out a company minus two platoons to find the enemy who had been firing mortars on Dau Tieng. The force killed one mortar team and captured a mortar and some small arms. The perimeter was quiet for days afterward, and the battalion concentrated on improving the perimeter of Dau Tieng that had been neglected by the soldiers of the Twenty-Fifth Infantry Division, who previously held the base camp.[41]

Chapter 2: Battalion Leadership

The following people took command of various units at this time:[5]

- Lt. Col. Newell Vinson, commander of 2/2 (Mech) June 9, 1969
- Capt. Richard Buckles, commander of A 2/2 (Mech) June 25, 1969
- Capt. Carrol Howard, commander of C 2/2 (Mech) July 7, 1969
- Maj. George Forrest, S-3 of 2/2 (Mech) July 9, 1969 (Had been XO)

July 1 at 12:00 p.m.

Joe Ladensack, or 2/6, has vivid memories of Maj. George Forrest. "After my in-country training at Di An, Headquarters of the First Infantry, I boarded a C-7 caribou aircraft and flew to Lai Khe. The first person I met was the 2/2 (Mech) XO Major George Forrest, who was waiting for me in his jeep. After welcoming me to the battalion, he drove me over to the Tactical Operations Center and sat me down for a briefing. I remember his soft voice and the attention he paid to me. He told me the battalion was up on Route 13 and in the town of An Loc. Thunder IV was their base. 'In the morning,' he said, 'you will take the convoy to

3

Thunder IV, and Lt. Col. James (Jacques) Michienzi, battalion commander, will assign you to either Alpha or Charlie Company.' Maj. Forrest went on to say that both Capt. Combs, Alpha Company CO, and Capt. Kelly, Charlie Company CO, were excellent teachers for young lieutenants. 'If you listen and learn you'll be okay. However,' said Forrest, 'they have very different teaching methods.'"

It was some twenty-three years later that 2/6 read *We Were Soldiers Once ... and Young*, by Lt. Gen. Harold G. Moore (Ret.) and Joseph L. Galloway and learned that Capt. George Forrest, as company commander of Alpha 1/5 Cavalry, had participated in the Ia Drang Valley Battle of LZ X-Ray. He was also deeply involved in the Battle of LZ Albany. "He was without a doubt the best officer that I served under in my brief army career," 2/6 stated unequivocally.[7]

New people to the battalion HHC were Capt. Tom Kelly, S-2 of 2/2 (Mech) as of July 7, 1969, who had been C 2/2 CO; and Maj. Jay McDivitt, XO of 2/2 (Mech) July 9, 1969, who graduated from the Citadel and was on his second tour in Vietnam. The first was also with the First Infantry Division.[1]

It was quite unusual to see this many new people in charge of a battalion, but with officers changing command on a six-month basis, which was common practice during an officer's twelve-month tour, there were always new people coming and going. Many soldiers couldn't even tell you the names of their officers because of the constant turnover.

Chapter 3: Actions in the Michelin

O n July 6, 1969, Second Platoon Alpha 2/2 (Mech) popped a bush (fired from an ambush) and inflicted casualties on the NVA. This was the first action for Capt. Buckles, and he was happy about it even though S. Sgt. Christopher was hit twice in the leg and had to be evacuated.[7]

Capt. Richard L. Buckles was twenty-seven years old and from Pacific Grove, California.[45] He had graduated from the Virginia Military Institute and was on his second tour in Vietnam. His prior tour had been with the 173rd Airborne Brigade, where he had commanded a platoon of tanks. He was well liked by his fellow officers, and they reported that they thought he was a competent, even-tempered officer who would be there when the fight started.[8] He may have been a little too nice, though, as he was much less of a disciplinarian than his predecessor, Capt. Dudley "Pete" Combs.

July 6 at 11:00 p.m.

The Second Platoon was headed by 2nd Lt. Joseph Ladensack, known as 2/6. He had gotten a BA degree from Arizona State University in Tempe, Arizona, in history with a minor in Oriental studies and had gone through ROTC. He also had an elementary knowledge of Mandarin Chinese, and he had been to jungle training in Panama. He was about four months ahead of his classmates in going to Vietnam.[7]

Pete Combs said, "Joe is one of the finest young lieutenants that ever wore the uniform and brave to a fault. Joe Ladensack to this day remains a little bit of an enigma to me. I just never saw anybody so brave and so quick all the time. Maybe Hugh Evans is the exception, but I wasn't there when Hugh first came in. Either those guys did not have any fear or they had somehow conquered it to an extent that I wish I could have conquered it."[43]

In his role as platoon leader, 2/6 won a Silver Star in the May battles and a Bronze Star in June, and he would win a second Silver Star before July was over. In all, he left Vietnam with two Silver Stars and six Bronze Stars. Many of the people in his platoon knew him only as 2/6. The "2" stands for Second Platoon, and the "6" means he was in command of it.[7]

Chapter 4: Movement to Tay Ninh

O n July 7, Alpha was told to join the battalion back at Dau Tieng and then move to Tay Ninh until the twentieth of July. The battalion would be placed under the operational control (op-con) of the First Brigade of the Twenty-Fifth Infantry Division.

July 7 at 12:00 p.m.

Bravo 2/2 (Mech) was assigned a "Rome plow security mission" in the Trapezoid Region. A Rome plow is a civilian bulldozer with a blade in the front that is used to knock down the jungle. The blades were made in Rome, New York. One recon platoon and the flame platoon, with four tracks that fired burning napalm rather than bullets, would stay at Dau Tieng for security. A "leg" company, B 1/2, commanded by Capt. Jerry Wilson, was assigned to the battalion as it moved toward Tay Ninh.[41]

Capt. Buckles briefed his platoon leaders, saying, "The attachment to the Twenty-Fifth Division is due to the belief that a major NVA offensive is expected around Tay Ninh, the third-largest city in South Vietnam, in order to disrupt the Paris peace talks. The battalion was to be based at Fire Support Base Buell, which was between Tay Ninh and Nui Ba Den.

Nui Ba Den, also known as the Black Virgin Mountain, was a large granite mountain on the plains northwest of Saigon. It had three peaks known as Nui Ba Den, Nui Cau, and Nui Dat. The last peak could not be seen except from the west, so most people thought there were only two peaks. The large one was Nui Ba Den and the smaller one was Nui Cau, which the Americans called the Little Sister.

Nui Ba Den rises 986 meters above sea level, while the town of Tay Ninh is only 15 meters above sea level and 10 klicks away. The Americans were told that the mountain got its name a thousand years earlier when some Vietnamese maidens leaped to their death off the mountain rather than to submit to the invading Chinese Army. It looks black from a distance because of the number of trees on it—hence its name, the Black Virgin Mountain.[7]

In writing his wife, Lt. Sergio Lugo of Charlie Company said, "By the way I'm going to send you some pictures of the Black Virgin Mountain, which is located here at Tay Ninh. It's possibly, I don't know if it's the highest point in Vietnam or what, but down here in the southern sector it is. Everything else is flat around there so you see it a long way away. It's three thousand feet high, and the first pictures I've taken are from about two thousand feet and you can spot it from Dau Tieng, which is something like ten miles away. You can spot it from Tay Ninh pretty easily. Well, Tay Ninh is right next door to it so that's the reason you don't have any difficulty spotting it. I remember at An Loc, we were 30 miles away and it stood out like a sore thumb. It's possibly the highest, like I said probably the highest landmark in southern Vietnam so it stands out pretty much. When you're close to it, it looks really huge. Clouds come over, it has a cloud cap on it most of the time and it's pretty."[35]

On the way to Tay Ninh, the front sprocket of the APC that SP4 Al Howard was driving fell off. He and his gunner, SP4 Sammy Labastida, had to return to Dau Tieng for repairs.[25]

Chapter 5: FSB Buell

About four thirty in the evening, the 2/2 (Mech) reached FSB Buell, which was situated between the Black Virgin Mountain and Tay Ninh. Charlie Company passed through it and established an RON site west of Buell. B 1/2 also went west of Buell and established a separate RON. Alpha 2/2 (Mech), the recon platoon, and battalion HQ took up positions inside of Buell. 2/6 noted that Buell was a very impressive fortification.

2/6 described it this way: "Buell had a large berm that was free of vegetation and trash. The berm had several layers of concertina wire in front of it and on top of it. The wire was in good shape. It was peppered with trip flares and all types of 'anti-intrusion devices.' The base perimeter was made up of infantry bunkers and 'hull defilade' tank and APC fighting positions. All the bunkers had 'Field of Fire' charts inside with claymore mine and 'Fougasse' detonators. It looked like a model you would find at Fort Benning."[7]

Years later 2/6 found a Twenty-Fifth Division newspaper article about a battle fought on August 18 and 19, 1968. An estimated NVA battalion had attacked FSB Buell. At one point in the battle, the NVA had breached the perimeter only to be driven off by artillery pieces firing directly into the invaders. "Buell was so well defended because it had to be!" 2/6 concluded.[7]

Lt. Col. Vinson was told that the Twenty-Fifth Infantry operated differently than the First. In the Twenty-Fifth, the Artillery had control of the Infantry. Vinson needed permission from the Artillery every time he wanted to move First Infantry Division troops. The Artillery could and did fire at any target they wanted to, at any time they wanted to, and they did not inform the infantry battalions when they were going on a fire mission. It was up to the infantry battalions to keep the artillery informed of the Infantry's position and to stay out of their way. Vinson was told that the United States had control of the top and the bottom of the mountain, but the Eighty-Eighth NVA Regiment had control of everything in between. The battalion and the Twenty-Fifth Infantry Division began a running battle over lack of support and correct battle tactics. Vinson noted that in the Twenty-Fifth Division, the brigade commander maneuvered companies, and the battalion commander maneuvered platoons.[25]

Chapter 6: Actions around FSB Buell

July 8 at 6:00 a.m.

After spending the night at Buell, Alpha Company began a routine that would be followed for the next few days. They conducted a "Mad Minute" before starting the day. A Mad Minute was one minute of continuous firing from every gun in the company at any enemy that might be trying to sneak up on the Americans. It also gave the infantry soldiers a chance to use up ammunition that may have pitted or magazines that had rusted. It was better to find out what maintenance needed to be done before going into battle.

Alpha then conducted a RIF (Reconnaissance in Force, formerly known as Search and Destroy) around Nui Ba Den and south of it to get some idea of the terrain. The men of Alpha noticed what looked like cooking fires on the side of the mountain.

Alpha 2/2 (Mech) set up a RON site at the "Old Fort" on the southeast side of Nui Ba Den. After they had set up their RON site, they watched F4's conduct bombing raids on the side of the mountain.

July 9 was again routine for the men. Alpha began the morning with a Mad Minute and then got ready to move out. On that day, they went north and west of the Black Virgin. They saw many signs of enemy activity. They saw trails in the elephant grass that indicated enemy movement leading toward the mountain. The battalion made note of this and made plans to send a platoon from Charlie Company on an ambush patrol the next night.[7]

July 9 at 7:00 a.m.

At the battalion level, an experienced S-3, Maj. Warne Mead, was assigned to head a joint American/South Vietnamese task force, and he was replaced by Maj. George Forrest. Maj. Forrest was a thirty-one-year-old from Leonardstown, Maryland. He attended Morgan State University and got his military commission through their ROTC program.[34]

Charlie Company was given the mission of going to Tay Ninh late in the afternoon. They were able to do some sightseeing and went by the magnificent temple of the Cao Dai religion. Cao Dai combines aspects of Buddhism, Hinduism, and Christianity[35]

On the tenth of July, Alpha conducted a Mad Minute and went out to RIF. They went twenty miles and went to see Cu Chi, the base camp of the Twenty-Fifth Infantry Division. It gained notoriety as a base camp that was built directly over the tunnels of the NVA they had been sent to find.

It was getting pretty confusing as to what we were doing there.[7]

That evening 1st Lt. Toney Mathews had a surprise for the NVA on the mountain. Mathews was a West Point graduate who was op-conned to Alpha 2/2 (Mech) as their Forward Observer. He was assigned to Delta Company 1/5 artillery, and it was his job to call in artillery whenever Alpha was in a firefight. He also worked with mortars, helicopters, and jets. His call sign was Daring 1. After serving in the military, Mathews had a career as a nuclear engineer.

July 10 at 7:00 a.m.

Mathews had been studying the mountain and had made some estimates of the locations of lights that had been seen the night before. On that night when the flashlights came on, Mathews called the Twenty-Fifth Artillery commander with the coordinates and asked for a zone and sweep. The Twenty-Fifth fired all six guns, moving left to right and top to bottom. In a few minutes, they had fired about three hundred rounds.[13]

Chapter 7: Dismounted RIF in the Jungle

July 11 at 7:30 a.m.

The morning of July 11, 1969, started out very normally. Alpha conducted a Mad Minute and then conducted a company dismounted RIF into a very thick jungle area. This was the first dismounted operation that any of the men of Alpha could remember. They were upset about it because they were mechanized infantry and had been trained to fight on tracks, not the ground.[7]

Pat McCoy was one of the platoon leaders for Bravo 1/2, First Infantry Division. Bravo Company 1/2, led by Capt. Jerry Wilson, had been op-conned to the 2/2 (Mech), and the battalion had been op-conned to the Twenty-Fifth Infantry Division. Bravo 1/2 had been on company-sized RIFs around the Black Virgin Mountain since the battalion had first gotten there.[28]

Around ten that morning, Charlie 2/2 (Mech) and Bravo 1/2 were both RIFing on the west side of the mountain. They crossed each other's path and Second Lieutenant Sergio J. Lugo of Charlie 2/2 (Mech) saw Second Lieutenant Pat Mc Coy of Bravo 1/2. They had been classmates at St. John's University in Minnesota, so they stopped to reminisce and catch up on other classmates who had also gone to Vietnam.[35]

Meanwhile, Alpha had a lot of problems. Lt. Williams (nicknamed Firefight on account of his mouth) got his platoon lost. They ran out of water, and many troops were overcome by heat. Capt. Buckles was not happy with the operation.[7]

Tennessee (he has asked that we use his nickname only) arrived for his first day at Alpha Company[32] along with PFC Robert Streightiff and George Kimmel. Kimmel was a twenty-one-year-old soldier from Cumberland, Maryland, who would not live through his second day in the field.[49]

Al Howard from Tennessee and his gunner, Sammy Labastida from California, were back in Dau Tieng repairing a sprocket on their APC. They went to the mountain as soon as the sprocket was fixed.[25]

That afternoon, A 2/2 (Mech), B 1/2, and C 2/2 (Mech) were given a briefing about the activities of the next day. B 1/2 would be helicoptered to the top of Nui Cau to do a Bomb Damage Assessment (BDA) and then RIF down the east side of the saddle between the two mountains. A 2/2 (Mech) would do a BDA at the bottom of the saddle between Nui Ba Den and Nui Cau and then set up as a blocking force in case B 1/2 chased the NVA off the mountain. C 2/2 (Mech) would RIF west of the mountain.[7]

Pat stated, "We were supposed to go up the back of the mountain, the side that had not been bombed before, and just look around. They said, 'They think there's something up there' and 'Try to push them down, if you can, into the tracks with the guns that would be waiting at the bottom.' As it worked out, we never did get helicoptered up there. We had to walk up because of the clouds at the top of the mountain."[28]

July 11 at 2:00 p.m.

When Alpha got back to the RON (Remain Overnight) site, there were a number of civilian Vietnamese outside the RON selling Cokes, ice, and haircuts. 1st Lt. Mike Mulhern, the mortar platoon leader, was in charge of the RON site, but when Capt. Buckles went looking for him, Capt. Buckles found him asleep. Capt. Buckles was very angry, yelling at both GIs and Vietnamese.

Capt. Buckles called a company formation and chewed out the company for about twenty minutes He said he had been told by the past company commander (Capt. Combs) that the company performed well in combat but could turn into a bunch of bandits if the captain looked the other way. Capt. Buckles said he would no longer be the "nice guy."[7]

Capt. Combs, the former Alpha Company commander, had just taken a position as the aide to Maj. Gen. Orwin C. Talbott, the commanding general of the First Infantry Division.[43]

Capt. Buckles spent the late afternoon taking pictures of the mountain. Several jets were hitting it with high explosives, white phosphorus (Willy Pete), and napalm bombs.[7]

Chapter 8: Mission for July 12, 1969

Around five thirty that evening, Capt. Buckles called the platoon leaders together for a briefing. These were his major points:

1. At about 11:30 p.m., the Air Force would conduct an Arc Light (B-52) Strike on the north side of the mountain in the saddle between Nui Ba Den and Nui Cau of the Black Virgin. This was targeted at a suspected concentration of the NVA.

July 11 at 5:30 p.m.

2. Alpha would have to move from the present RON site to the north since the B-52 strike would be conducted by radar. Alpha was to be at least 1.5 kilometers from the mountain for safety. Alpha would move right after the meeting.

3. The following morning, B 1/2 would perform an air assault from the top of the smaller peak (Nui Cau). Their mission was to sweep down the mountain and drive any NVA survivors off of it.

4. Alpha 2/2 (Mech) was to cordon off the bottom of the mountain and kill or capture any NVA that B 1/2 might drive down the mountain. The cordon would be made with the APCs.

5. Alpha 2/2 (Mech) would be ready to move out at first light but would move only on command of the

battalion. The battalion would coordinate the sealing of the Black Virgin from the air.

Alpha 2/2 (Mech) then moved to the new RON site in a large clearing about 1.6 klicks from the base of the mountain. Alpha dug their fighting positions deeper than normal to protect themselves from the Arc Light Strike. B 1/2 set up their RON about 1 1/2 klicks northwest of Nui Ba Den. PFC Bob Streightiff found himself on guard duty his first night in the company.[7]

Chapter 9: B-52 Strikes

That night at eleven thirty, Alpha watched the Arc Light Strike, consisting of two strikes of three aircraft each. Various comments follow by the men who watched the strike:

> "It was beyond belief. The ground shook; our ears hurt from the concussion, and we all dove for cover from debris that rained on the perimeter. The bombing lasted for about thirty minutes. My thoughts were of the poor bastards on the mountain."

> "It was quite spectacular. It was almost like living through an earthquake."

> "It was one of the most impressive things because you didn't hear anything right away. They woke us up at midnight, and the first thing we saw was an orange flash at the base of the hill and then another one, and they grew in a chain. It seemed to me— it looked like it went right up over the top of the hill and down the other side. It's like you're in an earthquake, a klick away, everything rattling and

shaking. It's one of the neatest things I've ever seen. Very impressive."

"We watched a magnificent fireworks display. They hit the entire side of the mountain. I still haven't seen anything to equal its awesomeness."

"I can remember the ground shaking. You felt the ground shake before you heard any noise, and then you looked up and the mountain was being rained on by bombs. It looked great, but we found out the next day that it didn't do much good."

"Oh, it shook the earth out from under us. Then the next morning, they sent us up there and the bombs didn't do nothing. The big bombs didn't do nothing except they knocked the trees out of the way. That mountain was some kind of granite or rock or something. Those bombs, all they did was burn it."[15]

After the bombing, Alpha saw several fires raging on the side of the mountain. They were much larger than the cooking fires that they had previously seen. It was speculated that the NVA were loading fifty-five-gallon drums of fuel into Nui Ba Den. Most of the men went to get some sleep, knowing that they would be in for a long day.[7]

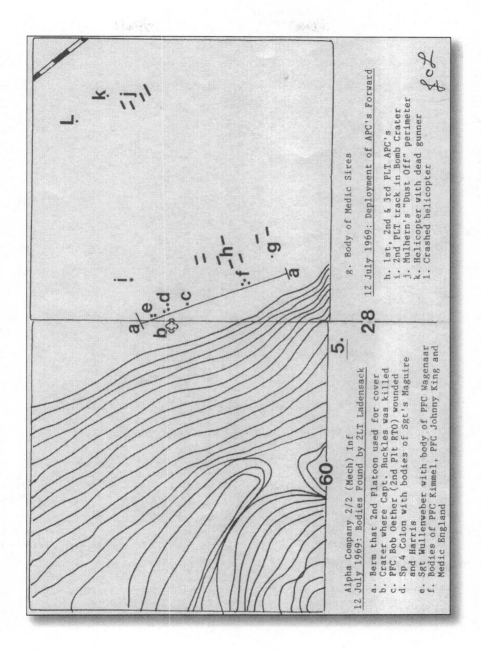

Alpha Company 2/2 (Mech) Inf
12 July 1969: Bodies Found by 2LT Ladensack

a. Berm that 2nd Platoon used for cover
b. Crater where Capt. Buckles was killed
c. PFC Bob Oether (2nd Plt RTO) wounded
d. Sp 4 Colon with bodies of Sgt's Maguire and Harris
e. Sgt Wullenweber with body of PFC Wagenaar
f. Bodies of PFC Kimmel, PFC Johnny King and Medic England

g. Body of Medic Sires

12 July 1969: Deployment of APC's Forward

h. 1st, 2nd & 3rd PLT APC's
i. 2nd PLT track in Bomb Crater
j. Mulhern's "Dust Off" perimeter
k. Helicopter with dead gunner
l. Crashed helicopter

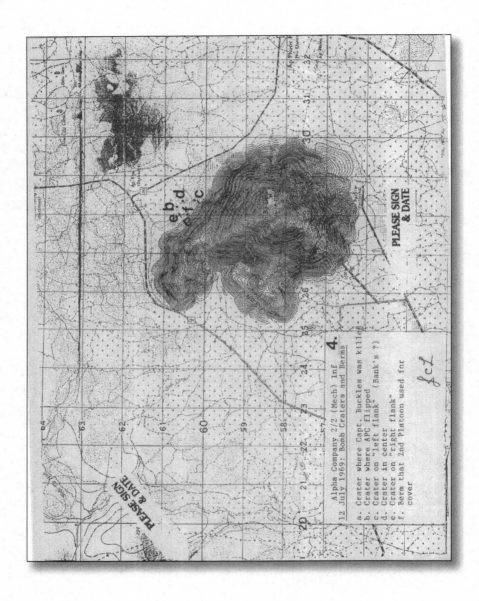

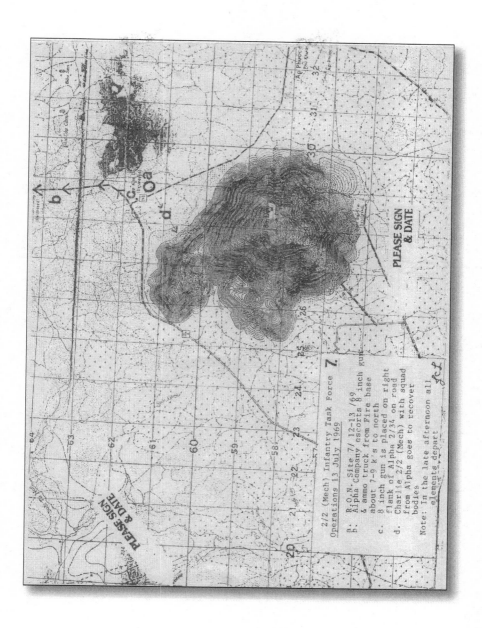

PLEASE SIGN & DATE

7.

2/2 (Mech) Infantry Task Force
Operations 13 July 1969

a: R.O.N. Site 7/12-13/69
b: Alpha Company escorts 8 inch gun
& ammo truck from Fire base
about 7-9 k's to north
c: 8 inch gun is placed on right
flank of Alpha 2/34 on road
d: Charlie 2/2 (Mech) with squad
from Alpha goes to recover
bodies

Note: In the late afternoon all
elements depart

19

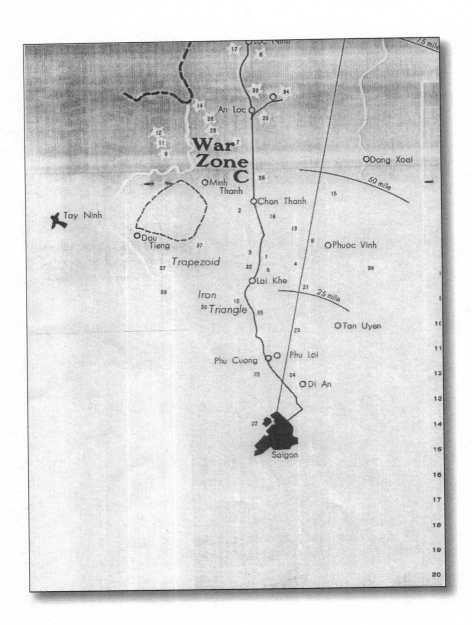

Loc Ninh
17   6
33   34
14   An Loc
26   20
25
12
11   War[7]
9   Zone
        C
        36
O Minh   O Dong Xoai
  Thanh
        O Chon Thanh   50 mile
        2   16   15
✈ Tay Ninh   13
O Dau   8   O Phuoc Vinh
  Tieng   37
    Trapezoid   3   1
27   32 5   4   36
        O Lai Khe   21
    Iron   10   25 mile
  30 Triangle   35
                23   O Tan Uyen
        Phu Cuong   O O Phu Loi
        25   24
                O Di An
        22
            Saigon

20

Sly & Moilanen, The Historical team May 23,1969
Photo credit: Bill Sly

FSB Buell, 7/12/69
Photo Credit: Marshal Prange

Charlie Company APC
Photo Credit: Coughennower

Cpt Buckles watching bombing run July 11
Photo Credit: Ladensack

25th Div Choppers leaving Niu Ba Den
Photo Credit: Coughennower

Alpha Co morning of 7/12
Photo Credit: Mulhern

25th Div General & Cpt Buckles 7/12
Photo Credit: Ladensack

A. Nui Ba Den after B 52 strike
B. Night bombing of Nui Ba Den by B 52s
C. Names of Alpha and Charlie Soldiers on the Wall
D. Bombed out area of Nui Ba Den
Photo Credits: Bill Sly

Lt Joe Ladensack with 2 Silver Stars and 6 Bronze Stars
Photo Credit: US Army Photo

Chapter 10: Change in Mission

At five the next morning, July 12, 1969, PFC Richard England,[47] the Second Platoon medic from Girard, Illinois, awoke to his twenty-first birthday. It was the last day of his life. He would die a hero.

Alpha had a stand-to, which meant that all soldiers had to be awake, dressed, and at their battle stations with weapons. There was no Mad Minute order given that day. Bravo 1/2 and C 2/2 also got ready for the day. Around a quarter after five, the order was given for Alpha to stand down, meaning that only the .50 gunners had to remain at the battle stations. The remaining troops would eat breakfast according to SOP.[7]

July 12 at 5:00 a.m.

1st Lt. James Brezovec of Charlie Company said, "The first thing in the morning of July 12, 1969, we were at Fire Support Base Buell, the one right out in the boonies out to the west. It sat on the middle of an open plain out on the west side of the mountain."[30]

PFC Robert Streightiff says, "I was new to Vietnam. I got in country on June 10, and I arrived in the field at Alpha Company on July 11. The challenging thing was going out the day before. I didn't know anybody."[17]

At six, the order was given for Alpha to mount up, meaning that all soldiers were mounted on APCs with weapons at the ready and all radios were logged onto their net. All soldiers had to have full battle dress: helmets, flak jackets, and ammo pouches. At the order to move out, the APCs would move into the proper battle formation, usually a four-by-four. The normal four-by-four formation was a square with four tracks to a side and the headquarters unit in the middle. At that time, a thick fog surrounded the area, and there was no order to move out.

2Lt Gene Giancola, First Platoon leader, who had been a former NCO before receiving his commission from Officer Candidate School, woke up with stomach problems and was helicoptered out of the company later that day. SFC Charles Steward moved up to platoon leader. SFC Steward was an experienced platoon sergeant who had been in Vietnam for some time. This was his second tour, and he was well liked by the men.[33] He was thought of as an old man even though he was probably thirty-seven.[14]

There were several other people missing that day. The XO, 1Lt Hugh O. Evans, was in Hong Kong on R&R. Hugh Evans had been an amateur boxer in the lighter divisions. After his time in the army, he became a lawyer specializing in representing other lawyers who had been sued because someone thought they hadn't been represented properly. 1st Sergeant Jimmy Thomas, who had been promoted while serving with Alpha and was awarded seven awards while he served there, was back at Dau Tieng taking care of administrative matters. S. Sgt. James Bondsteel, who was awarded a Medal of Honor for his actions at An Loc; Cecil Sawyer, the captain's RTO; Dennis Difalco; and Bob Douglas (Porky) were all on R&R.[6] SP4 Tim Frake, who had been wounded at An Loc and was returning to his company, was at Fire Support Base Buell and spent the day loading ammo into helicopters during the battle.[6]

An hour later, Capt. Buckles informed the platoon leaders over the radio that there were some problems with B 1/2 and that they could not get up the mountain. Alpha was to stand down but be ready to move out at a moment's notice. "Stand down" meant that all nondrivers and .50 gunners could get off the tracks and get out of the sun. The APC engines would be shut down.[7]

Early that same morning, SP4 John R. (Jack) Heick of C 2/2 received his mail. In it was a "Dear John" letter from his girl in Illinois. Jack began crying and could not finish the letter. A friend, SP4 Robert E. Worrell, a twenty-year-old soldier from Portsmouth, Virginia, nicknamed Squirrel,[55] read the letter out loud. Squirrel was a .50 gunner who was short and had a good sense of humor. He was an outgoing type of guy. Jack's ex signed the letter, "Die for it." The next day, Squirrel was killed.[37]

The battalion log reads, "0803–Charlie Horse 41, an A-1 skyraider, reported 3/55 gal. drums on Nui Ba Den, trail activity, tunnels, evidence of something being dragged into tunnels after bomb strike."[1]

July 12 at 6:45 a.m.

By 8:25 a.m., Bravo 1/2 and Alpha 2/34 (Tanks) linked up and were moving. The Bravo 1/2 Company commander, Capt. Jerry Wilson, had been told by Lt. Col. Vinson that he was to make a BDA on the west side of Nui Cau and climb to the top. The helicopters had been diverted because of the fog on the mountain, so the troops were going up on foot.[1]

Second Lt. Pat McCoy remembers, "We started out on the morning of the twelfth about eight thirty in the morning. We kind of walked up the north side. I'm kind of glad we didn't take helicopters as there was no place for the choppers to put down. They would have had to hover, and then we would have had to jump out. I once fell into a crevasse that way and messed up my back. We went up that way and then they wanted us to come down the east side. We never did get over the saddle. Part of the company got to the top around one o'clock in the afternoon. My platoon was in the middle of the formation, and we never got there.

27

We could see where the bombs had hit the day before. The bombs didn't seem to hurt the mountain at all, but [they] sure mowed down the trees. There was all rock on the east side of the mountain. We went up on the west side where there was still trees. It wasn't as dense as a jungle as we'd been in other places, but it was still jungle."[28]

At eight thirty Alpha 2/2 moved out for a BDA of the base of the mountain. When they got to the road, Capt. Buckles deployed the mortar platoon on the east side of it and continued on toward the mountain.[8]

Lt. Col. Vinson said, "I got on a loach to make a visual inspection of the damage to the mountain The pilot came very close to the mountain, and we were able to see the entire area of the Arc Light. We were close enough to the mountain to smell the odor of death; however, there were no bodies in sight and no fire coming from the mountain."[41]

July 12 at 8:35 a.m.

According to the battalion log, "At 8:50 -B 1/2 (Infantry) and 2/34 (M48/A/3 Tanks) in position and proceeding with operations. At 9:05 - 4.2 meters (Mortars) and scouts loc 237599."[1]

Around nine thirty, Alpha reached the base of the mountain. They found bomb craters, punji pits, and booby traps, but no NVA. They returned to a location one klick east of the saddle between the mountains.[7]

At nine forty-five, a Cobra (helicopter gunship) from the 1/4 Cavalry, First Infantry Division (Blue Max), reported "1 VC Vin 280592, engaging," according to the battalion log.[1]

Banks says, "The next morning we were put in a blocking position. As time rolled on, it was time for the leg unit to come rolling down from the top of the mountain, and nothing happened."[19]

Capt. Buckles called a briefing of his platoon leaders to his track. He stated that the mission had been called off. (This was incorrect.) Capt. Buckles instructed his platoon leaders to reestablish the RON site. According to company SOP, this meant they would put up RPG screens, redig fighting positions, conduct APC maintenance, and clean weapons. Soldiers could take off their flak jackets and shirts.[7]

The battalion log states, "At 10:00 -Blue Max 27 confirms 1 KBH (Killed by Helicopter) xt 280592- Khaki uniform."[1]

A platoon of five Patton M48A3 tanks came down the road on the east side of Nui Ba Den and stopped near the 81-millimeter mortars of Alpha Company. They faced their big guns toward the mountain.[8]

July 12 at 10:00 a.m.

The Twenty-Fifth Division's Col. Hayward landed at the mortar platoon location and asked Mulhern where the rest of the company was. The colonel stated, "The 2/2 is working for me now."[8]

According to the battalion log at 10:25, "Blue Max reports @ 258602 trail coming down from mountain with recent heavy use. Blue Max leaving station."[1]

After securing their area, Alpha Company, Second Platoon, received permission from Capt. Buckles to pass a football around.[7] Jim Hale says, "We were kinda relaxed. When I saw a helicopter overhead, I thought to myself, 'This is going to piss someone off. We don't look professional.'"[26]

Alpha Company had an officer-versus-enlisted volleyball game at the Dau Tieng base camp on the Fourth of July.

29

"I remember a huge crowd all cheering for the enlisted team," recalls Ladensack. "Capt. Buckles later stated that we should have more events like this to boost morale. I wanted to create a flag football team in the Second Platoon and challenge the other platoons. July 12 ended up being our first and last practice."[7]

Col. Post at Buell was the First Brigade commander from the First Infantry Division. Forrest says, "Now, what was Col. Post doing on the net other than protecting his interest because there was not a lot of understanding and cooperation between the commanders of the unit that we were attached to in Twenty-Fifth Infantry Division. There was constant battle going on about support and lack of support and so forth."[34]

Chapter 11: The General's Visit

A Huey with Twenty-Fifth Division markings landed outside the RON site of Alpha 2/2 (Mech). A one-star general (Brig. Gen. Davis Henderson) and two officers got out. Capt. Buckles greeted them and took them to his track. We have found no one who heard the conversation directly, but here are some of the comments made by the soldiers after the meeting.[74]

July 12 at 11:00 a.m.

Banks says, "The next thing was a chopper from the Twenty-Fifth landed and some people got out and talked to our captain. The conversation was very loud, and the one-star waved his arms a lot. After about ten minutes, BG Henderson left and his party got back into their helicopter."[19]

"Capt. Buckles was mad after the conversation. He was upset at the general, in a sense; the general interfered in our business."[19]

S. Sgt. Phil Deering says, "When Williams came back from talking to the captain, the only word we got was we were attached to the Twenty-Fifth, and they had been going up in there and getting into some trouble every once in a while, so why it got assigned to us, I'm not really sure. That's what's really strange. And so we were going to go up that thing and why—I don't have a bloody idea. What the hell. And we were just going to take this direct path right up there. We never even scouted the area around there. That was really strange."[20]

"What I was told was that the general stated, 'You don't get anything by waiting, so we are sending you up the mountain. I want a body count.'"[19]

"I didn't hear the conversation, but word went through the company like wildfire before we went up the hill; everybody knew it. It wasn't something we heard afterwards. It was something we knew before—instantly. Even before being briefed we knew we were to walk up the mountain."[11]

Pete Combs says, "If indeed any brigade commander ordered Capt. Buckles to dismount and climb up, it was a very bad order. Now the reason for that is the company commander of a mechanized infantry company should be the one to decide when he should dismount and when he should not dismount. Now I understand that somebody's going to say that I am probably wrong and that I don't have this in very clear perspective, but I will tell you that I was a mechanized infantry commander for seven months and that I was for about ten and a half months (my first year) a straight-leg platoon leader and Company XO. The real difference between somebody who was successful as a mechanized infantry company commander in that environment and somebody who was not successful was knowing when to mount and when to dismount the troops.

That was the difference between taking casualties and not taking casualties. That's the first point. The second point is very clearly this: Going up on the mountain after an enemy—and I said this then, I've said it many times before, and I will say it now—any time in that war you went after an enemy on his own turf, particularly when he was high and you were below, you were making a mistake. We didn't need that piece of terrain; we didn't need to kill an extra ten enemy or something like that. It wasn't really accomplishing a mission. The most startling example, in that war, was the taking of Hamburger Hill and then the retaking of Hamburger Hill. We didn't need the terrain. If they were there, the best thing to do was just bomb the living shit out of them and let them stay there and then nailing them when they came off the mountain."[43]

A member of Alpha says, "We were mechanized infantry. We didn't go for that shit."

Before the reader views the prior statement as either insubordination or skepticism, a short account of the history and development of armored combat in Vietnam is necessary. This history is contained in *Vietnam Studies: Mounted Combat in Vietnam*, by Gen. Donn A. Starry and published by the Department of the Army in 1978. Gen. Starry states that at the start of the war, US senior officers viewed armored combat through the lens of the French experience in the Indochina War. Therefore, there was an extreme reluctance to introduce armored formations into Vietnam, and the policy of "no tanks in the jungle" took a firm foothold.

After Maj. Gen. Jonathan O. Seaman's tank and mechanized units were taken from him before the deployment of the First Infantry Division to Vietnam in 1965, he firmly requested that at least his ground reconnaissance unit, the First Squadron, Fourth Cavalry (Quarter Cav) be deployed. After considerable resistance from the army staff in Washington, the request was granted but only for test purposes. Even then, upon arriving in Vietnam, Gen. Westmoreland ordered all of the Quarter Cav's tanks (M48A3s) be withdrawn and held in a motor pool in Phu Loi.

The Quarter Cav immediately began to develop tactics and maneuvers suited for combat in Vietnam. At the Battle of Ap Bau Bang (November 11–12, 1965), a task force of the Second Battalion, Second Infantry (Dismounted Infantry) and Troop A, less nine tanks still at Phu Loi, made a definite case for the use of armored forces at least for the First Infantry Division.

When Maj. Gen. William E. De Puy became division commander of the Big Red One, he began experimental operations with the Quarter Cav. Now with their M48A3 tanks assigned, there were major successes at the Battles of Ap Tau O (June 8, 1966), Highway 13 near Srok Dong and Minh Thanh Road (July 9, 1966). Maj. Gen. De Puy requested that the Second Battalion, Second Infantry, be mechanized. This was completed on January 1, 1967. These units continued developing new tactics from lessons learned. The 2/2 Mech soon began to refer to themselves not as the "Ramrods" but as "The Iron Fist of the Big Red One."

In the First Infantry Division, this developed into a new concept of armored warfare. Armored units were now part of a combined arms team—armor, armored cavalry, infantry, artillery, air units, and mechanized infantry. The M113A1 morphed from a "battle taxi" deploying infantry short of the objective to an infantry fighting vehicle that allowed infantry to ride the vehicles until they were on top of the objective. Simply stated, the infantry changed to become "Panzergrenadiers" (German-mounted infantry in WWII) that were part of the blitzkrieg. All training in that role took place at the unit level in Vietnam. Soldiers and officers trained in official army doctrine developed for the plains of Europe were introduced to a concept totally foreign when they arrived in Vietnam. One battalion commander noted that he would rather have completely new soldiers than have those from Fort Knox and Fort Benning in the United States and the Fulda Gap in Germany, who had to be totally retrained.

Therefore, one could understand the reaction of the young soldier who had been indoctrinated in Vietnam in a totally new concept. His ability to be an 11-B infantryman had been diminished in his normal functioning by skill set, but more importantly, (psychologically) enhanced by the new tactics developed at the platoon and company level.[7]

"We weren't equipped to hit that mountain anyway. We were a mechanized outfit. The general flew over and seen that we weren't busy, and he met Capt. Buckles and told us to hit the mountain. And that's when the mistake was made."[32]

Banks says, "The company commander called the RTOs and told them to have the platoon leaders come to his track for a meeting, and the lieutenant came back and told us to saddle up because we were going up the mountain."[19]

The old man was red in the face and spoke in a speech pattern that showed that he was upset. He stated that the general was the commander of the unit of the Twenty-Fifth Division that Alpha was op-conned to and was upset that Alpha was "running around like a bunch of wild Indians." Capt. Buckles reported that Alpha had a new mission. The general stated (incorrectly) that since B 1/2 could not come down the mountain, Alpha 2/2 (Mech) would move up the mountain to do a BDA. Capt. Buckles told his platoon leaders to be ready to move out at 1130 hours with the Second Platoon leading and followed by the Third and the First. Capt. Buckles said that they were leaving the mortar platoon in place, and they would be leaving the drivers and gunners on the tracks, but they were to remain in place. He also stated that he had placed a radio call into Lt. Col. Vinson and said, "Maybe he won't think walking up a hill is such a good idea."[7]

Vinson landed his helicopter northwest of the mountain and met with Maj. Ezikih of the Twenty-Fifth Infantry Division. Maj. Ezikih told Vinson that his battalion was to make a BDA of the area. Vinson explained that he has just done that by air and that no bodies had been found. Ezikih informed Vinson that it was to be done on foot, but Vinson objected to the order. He said, "I'm not going to send any of my people up there to do that when I don't think that the objective is worth it, to risk people like that." Maj. Ezikih was adamant that a BDA must be done on foot.[41]

July 12 at 11:16 a.m.

Lt. Col. Vinson repeated, "I don't accept that. Call Col. Hayward and tell him I don't want to do that. However, if we do have to make that BDA, I do have B 1/2 on top of Nui Cau, and they can come down from the top."

Maj. Ezikih came back and said, "You have to dismount Alpha 2/2 (Mech); they have to go up on foot." Lt. Col. Vinson said, "I refuse to do that without a direct order to do so."

Maj. Ezikih went back to the radio and after a short conversation and stated, "Colonel Hayward gives you a direct order to dismount Alpha 2/2 and go up that hill."[41]

Forrest says years later, "The fact that a Twenty-Fifth Division general was in Alpha company is something I've heard for the first time. I did not know until you just told me that that is, in fact, what happened—that there was a general officer on the ground. Now I do know that Twenty-Fifth Infantry Division had a habit of having these guys all over and they were in and out of our areas of operation, doing lots of stuff, because we had had a prior incident of that."[34]

Around eleven thirty, Lt. Col. Vinson informed Capt. Buckles that he was to make a dismounted BDA of the saddle area of Nui Ba Den. Lt. Col. Vinson expected that the company commander would dismount one squad, move the tracks up as close to the mountain as possible, and make the BDA in that manner, using the .50 guns to recon by fire over the heads of the five to ten men going up the saddle.[41]

By then the lead elements of B 1/2 had reached the top of Nui Cau. McCoy's platoon was in the center of the company and never reached it. The First Platoon began taking fire from the east side of the saddle.

Vinson told Capt. Jerry H. Wilson, the company commander of B 1/2, to dismount Nui Cau down the northwest side of the mountain as A 2/2 company was climbing up from the east. McCoy was told that the enemy was seen on Nui Ba Den and that another company would engage. B 1/2 decided to get off of the mountain fast. An order came over the radio, "Get your ass off the mountain."[38]

Lt. Williams, the Third Platoon Leader of A 2/2, met with his platoon and told them to saddle up; they were going up the mountain because the Twenty-Fifth Infantry general had ordered them to. The old-timers complained because the 2/2 was a mechanized unit and it had been trained to fight on the tracks, not on the ground. SP4 Chip Banks says, "I am with the Third Platoon, first track. Lt. Williams is our platoon leader, and I am his RTO." [19]

Doc D says, "I wasn't told what to do that day. Normally Top would fill us in, but he wasn't there that day. I was just following along with whatever Headquarters did. We were told that we were going to assault, evidently people didn't dream that we were going to make contact. After that B-52 strike, we thought we were going to see if there was anything we could clean up." [11]

Some of the guys had heard about the Black Virgin Mountain and had been told that it was a stronghold of the VC and the NVA regulars. Many were upset at the Twenty-Fifth general for sending them on this mission. It was reported that the general didn't like them "sitting around."

July 12 at 11:24 a.m.

Bob Strightiff states, "We were very angry that we had to dismount and head for the battle. We weren't trained for that. Sgt. Jerry Campbell came back and told us to saddle up. As a new guy, I didn't have any idea what the hell I was doing that day." [17]

I also called the Second Platoon around me. "We have been ordered up the mountain to see what damage the B-52s did last night," I began. "Capt. Buckles doesn't think that the APCs can drive on the mud, and nobody wants them to get stuck." The men nodded in agreement, as unsticking an APC was one of the least favorite activities of Mech infantry. [7]

"We will be going in dismounted, and we will be in the lead as we are Alpha's best platoon." The men laughed as they remembered what had happened to the Third Platoon the day before. I then listed what would be the basic load for the operation. "I want everyone to take at least two canteens of water, twenty magazines of M-16 ammunition (four hundred rounds), and at least one field dressing. We'll take the M-60 MG with us and three men to carry extra 7.62 MG belts. I don't think we'll be gone long enough for food, but carry one C ration meal if you want a snack—but only one meal as water is the highest priority. Also the M-79 gunner will stay with me at all times. Bring mostly Willy Pete rounds so you can mark any targets." I concluded with, "Staff Sergeant Hill and I will have an inspection in ten minutes."[7]

I then went to brief the APC drivers and gunners. They were to remain alert—absolutely no Vietnamese civilians should be in the area—and monitor the company net as to the progress of the mission. "Stand by to move to the base of the mountain when ordered." That order still resonates in my mind. That may have been the only order that made any sense that day.[7]

Chapter 12: No Place to Hide

Shortly before noon, Capt. Buckles radioed the platoon leaders and said that Lt. Col. Vinson had ordered Alpha to make a dismounted assault on the mountain. This was only the second dismounted mission that members of Alpha could remember. The first was the day before.[7]

Within half an hour, A 2/2 left for a dismounted assault on Nui Ba Den. Sgt. Calvin Maguire, a twenty-one-year-old soldier from Altoona, Pennsylvania, who was on his second tour, was in charge of the very first squad to proceed toward the mountain.[57] He told PFC Maurice Gilliam and

Sgt. Hennes to take point. S. Sgt. Cantor Hill, a man on his second tour, was in charge of the tail element of Second Platoon, and SP4 Lee Stember was given the assignment of training a new M-60 gunner.[7] They moved out with Third Platoon. Banks says, "So they put us semi on line going up. It was Second Platoon, First Platoon, and Third Platoon, like that, going up. We were not spread out too much on line, probably twenty men across. At the base of the mountain, it was real thick jungle and then it opened up to a kind of grassy area. And at the very bottom of the mountain, it opened up into a sandy area."[19]

SP5 Elmer Dehaven, "Doc D," says, "We assaulted up that mountain. We didn't normally do this, as we were a mechanized unit. When we did dismount, we would walk behind our tracks through the rubber plantation or the bamboo. This time we left the tracks about three football fields behind. They were back so far you couldn't yell for them to come up."[11]

The drivers and .50 gunners were to remain with the tracks, so the total company, including the command group, would have been about sixty-five to seventy men. The order of march that day was Second Platoon, Command group, Third Platoon, and then First Platoon.[7]

Hale says, "Well, all I could hear was mumbling amongst the troops saying that this is bullshit, to walk up a mountain when we're mechanized. I heard that we were having to RIF up a mountain because the general can't stand to see us sit around. We heard that there was another company that was going to RIF down and we were going to RIF up and meet, but it never happened. I heard that when the men got to the bottom of the mountain there was just no cover." Hale was one of the few people that had been trained for his position. He went to Fort Knox to learn how to drive an APC and fire the .50 machine gun. The drivers and gunners turned to the company net to hear what was happening.[26]

SP4 Van Morrison (Van), a driver who had actually been trained on how to drive an APC, and SP4 Ray Coursen (Hippie), the gunner of the medic track, began to wait for further developments. SP4 Earl Hebert from Port Aransas, Texas, came over to their track and began to play a new tape that he had gotten, "Some Kind of Drag." He would be wounded before the day was over. They do not remember anyone being in charge of their group of drivers and gunners.[14]

On January 8, 1969, an airplane left America headed for Vietnam by way of Alaska and Japan[14]. It was full of young men heading off to war. Although they didn't know it yet, thirteen of them would go to Alpha 2/2 (Mech). Two of these thirteen were Ray Coursen (Hippie) and Van Morrison. These two people came from very different backgrounds, and yet by sharing the experience of war together, they became lifelong friends.

In early July, Van was asked to drive the medic track that Top rode on when he was in the field. According to Van, "I started politicking immediately for Ray to be my .50 gunner. When I got the track, I found out the gunner was going home too, and I wanted someone that I knew would be there in a fight. As far as I'm concerned, Hippie was the best gunner in the company."[14]

2/6 was losing Second Platoon's best driver and gunner, but 1st Sgt. Thomas had already made his decision. 2/6 thought it was advantageous to have a good relationship with the crew of the medic track.[7]

The dismounted Alpha started toward the mountain and entered a wooded area. The company walked in two columns, but they were spread out. The wooded area was not as thick as the Bo Loi Woods, but it slowed them down. Soon Alpha came to an area of sparse woods and then a road. After the road, Alpha came upon another heavily wooded area followed by a small clearing. After crossing another group of small woods, Alpha came upon a rice paddy and then some medium woods with some heavy woods off to the south side. In this set of woods, Alpha first came upon bomb craters that they assumed were from the B-52s the night before. One of the columns came upon a deserted NVA camp that probably held a platoon. There was still a little smoke from the fire.

July 12 at 12:17 p.m. About one hundred meters from the base of the mountain, Alpha came across elephant grass, and just at the base of the mountain was a foot trail that looked like a berm. The elephant grass was about four or five feet tall. This area was shaped like an oval one hundred meters by three hundred meters, with the mountain in front of them and trees to the left and behind.

As the platoon marched toward the mountain, 2/6 paid special attention to the ground. It was moist but could easily support the weight of an APC. 2/6 thought, *Why the hell didn't we bring them along?* But then he snapped back to the mission, thinking, "I have to keep myself as alert as the men of Second Platoon were. I am proud of my men's performance thus far."[7]

Alpha rushed the trail using fire and maneuver techniques. They observed that the mountain was covered with heavy boulders, most of them the size of an APC but some of them the size of a house. The trees in the area had all been blown away by the B-52 strikes, so the enemy had a

41

very good field of fire. The mountain was very steep, and there were few ways up. Walking around the boulders was extremely difficult, and the soldiers immediately lost visual contact with one another. Banks says, "When we got to the base of the mountain, we couldn't go up spread out because we couldn't get through. It was kind of closed in through the rocks and crevasses."

Alpha 2/2 (Mech) began climbing the mountain in the following order: Second Platoon was the highest and the farthest to the left. Capt. Buckles and his RTO, Mike Mirenda,[12] with Toney Mathews and his RTO, Frank Lawrence, and Third Platoon were in the middle and had started to find a trail up the mountain.[13] Lee Stember noticed that his trainee was having a lot of trouble climbing the mountain and holding the gun.[18] First Platoon was on the right and had not begun to climb.[7]

Sgt. Maguire of Second Platoon had found a tunnel opening. 2/6 reported this to Capt. Buckles and was told to check it out. He dropped a grenade into the opening, and it appeared that the grenade exploded deep inside the mountain before it hit bottom. Mathews, Buckles, and Gilliam also began finding a significant number of caves.[7] They also threw in grenades. Gilliam remembers that the grenades dropped a long way because he could barely hear the explosions. They sounded like they were still in the tunnels.[24]

Tennessee continues, "We took off for the mountain until we came up to this little tree line. We was then walking down a little walkway over a ditch. We went across that in single file, and as we took toward the mountain we just sorta went across along the foot of the mountain. We were parallel with the mountain. They was supposed to have dropped foot soldiers at the top of the hill; I don't think they ever dropped them. So, they kind of left us holding the bag. I was about ten to fifteen people from the rear, and when there was about two to three left, that's when they opened up."[16]

Banks, the Third Platoon's RTO, heard a *thump, thump, thump.* It was later determined that the NVA were shooting RPGs that were hitting the soft sand of the trail and not exploding.[19] Then one of the RPGs exploded, just missing SP4 Roger (Ram-Jet) Hulsey and hitting Sgt. Bob Hall in the legs.[22] The NVA opened up with small-arms fire also. Those on the mountain dove for cover and began to return fire, while those at the base of the mountain tried to find whatever cover was available. Bob Streightiff noticed snipers in the trees shooting at them from behind. Bob stated, "We were basically just sitting ducks."[17]

July 12 at 12:55 p.m. Doc D says, "The NVA waited until part of our group was on the mountain, and then they opened up on us. I was in the second element going up, and we hadn't gotten to the mountain. When we first got hit, we lowered ourselves down into a punji pit. We just kicked the punjis over and let ourselves down in. We stayed there for—I don't know how long—until the tracks came up for the first time. See, when we went back up the mountain, it was after the initial part of the battle. We went to get whoever was left on the mountain."[11]

Capt. Howard, the West Point grad who was on his first tour of Vietnam and the Charlie Company commander, says, "I don't remember the exact time of day, but we were operating in the vicinity. The whole battalion was in the same vicinity, and I knew they were participating in an operation in conjunction with a company from the Twenty-Fifth Division on Nui Cau. The Twenty-Fifth was supposed to go in from the top, air assault, and then assault down

43

from the top, and another company was supposed to come up from the bottom and they were going to meet in the middle to kind of purge the area."

"My mission was different that day but to be in the vicinity, and I was monitoring the battalion frequency. Somewhere around lunchtime or just after lunchtime, things started to sound pretty disjointed. We were on a search and destroy mission, just kind of looking around scouting the area seeing what was what. I can remember that it sounded like things weren't going well from the very beginning, and I had a little latitude in where I could operate, so I began to move toward the mountain of my own volition; it just seemed like a good idea in case there was trouble."[29]

Roger (Ram-Jet) got his nickname because he was a tunnel rat; he went into a lot of enemy tunnels. There's a cartoon character named Roger Ram-Jet who does the same thing. SP4 Donavan Kollness looked like a bulldog, so his nickname became Spike.[23]

Sgt. David Anderson, nicknamed Popcorn, said, "We were one of the few from First Platoon that got on the mountain. We got up fifty to a hundred meters or so. We were there for a half hour, maybe an hour. It seemed like we stopped as something was happening above us. It was then that the enemy opened up on us. The first shot they fired at us that day was a rocket-propelled grenade. We were sitting around the bomb crater. I remember watching it fly straight toward me, but there was nothing I could do. It came way too quickly. I did not even have time to yell, holler, duck, or even move."[23]

Spike says, "I was sitting inside the crater, near the right side of it. The round flew past my head, missing me by only a couple of feet. The RPG landed in the soft, light-colored, clay-like dirt created by the B-52 blast. It landed right between Bob Hall's legs and exploded. The soft dirt helped to shield the blast, but that wasn't enough. The explosion literally blew the pants almost completely off of Hall. He took a piece of shrapnel in his left calf."[23]

Popcorn says, "We were sitting on the lip of the crater and were tossed from the crater, some ten to fifteen feet in the air. It was mass confusion. We scrambled for cover, but there was none to be found except a small tree that had somehow escaped the bombing the night before."[23]

S. Sgt. Phil Deering says, "After the B-52 strike, we didn't expect anything to be there. We were just amazed at it. It was just like a big fireworks display going on. The ground shook and everything, and then we thought, 'What the hell. We're going up here for now,' and then we get to those damn big, old boulders. We thought, 'This is stupid.' First we come across this field, we get in these boulders and to tell you the truth, we were whispering, it was going up and down through the line because you, basically, had this kind of a stupid ass line going, zig zagging across and it was going up through the line like, you know what, my ass's grass if they start firing at us. We were on line, a semiline, you might say. That's, basically, the way we kind of went up."[20]

Forrest said, "I had no idea. You're me giving information that I'm hearing for the first time. Once the fight started, I remember that, because we had assumed that they were out of position and again, unable to communicate, because at that point, we had gotten a bunch of folk from Twenty-Fifth Infantry Division and Colonel Post had come in. They had Vinson outside to talk about if he was needed to get up there to do some things. I'm not sure what he did from there. I know that I was left in the CP (Command Post),in the dark, kind of with all this radio silence. I know all the time that there's a big firefight going on out there," Forrest recounted. "I can hear it because with all the RTOs and whatever that was in the area, whenever a mike was keyed, I could hear it. I mean, the confusion of what's going on and what you think is an orderly battle, with orders being given and guys being maneuvered to do whatever, I know that didn't happen up there."[34]

Phil recounted, "You know what? Somehow, most of us decided for ourselves because it just seems like we didn't hesitate. One took this spot; one took the other because it was like one whole platoon. We got separated. When we got separated, actually the platoons got separated. There was not even any of the coordination of fire or base to fire even a way up the mountain. There was like maybe six or seven or two or three places because the rocks were so heavy, so big. We had to kind of get around them, and we'd go around one and there'd be somebody you'd never seen before coming up with you and then the two of you, you'd follow each other, so it was no longer in platoon or no longer in squad formation and we lost track of each other."[20]

Spike said, "I was in the bomb crater lighting a cigarette when the second RPG hit. My M-16 was draped across my lap, and I lost it and my helmet immediately. The blast hit my claymore mine ammo bag, which was on my left hip. It ripped the bag wide open. If the bag wouldn't have been there, the blast could have hit me and could have wounded me badly. The explosion tossed me into the air and launched me over fifteen feet. I landed on some wait-a-minute vines that were near the crater's edge. At first I didn't know how I got there; I just knew that I had to get out."[22]

The battalion log states, "1:00 PM - Alpha 2/2 in contact. Light fire teams requested."[1]

Phil says, "When Jerry Campbell came over here as a regular infantryman and so forth,; he was a real conscientious guy about his job, probably more conscientious than most guys were, to tell you the truth. Did what he was told. Didn't question as much, and he put—whatever he did, he put 110 percent in almost constantly. We made him a sergeant and gave him a squad. Here was a guy that did 100 percent, 110 percent all the time. Most guys had a hard time doing 100 percent but Jerry always did 110 percent, so we really had somebody to look up to and Jerry had a hard time understanding anyone that didn't give 110 percent."[20]

Jerry says, "Well, the only thing I'm saying is single file, I think, we about all got there at the same time, and that's when they opened up on us. And that's the only thing I remember, and when somebody opens up, what the hell you do? There's not much you can do. You can't hit somebody you can't even see, you know, so, well, the order was given. Hell, everybody might as well try to get off because you can't do anything where you're at."[33]

Phil says, "When the battle started, I was up probably maybe fifty, sixty yards up, and it wasn't ten, fifteen minutes after I first started climbing. It was like they waited for the last guy to get on the mountain."[20]

The NVA opened up with small-arms fire and RPGs, and the main body of Alpha quickly became pinned down. First Platoon was down in the grass with no protection, while the rest had boulders the size of houses. The NVA were right on top of the Second and Third Platoons with estimations of sixty to two hundred feet. It was also estimated that the enemy force was between fifty and two hundred people.[7]

Hall says, "The explosion caused me to lose my helmet and M-16 rifle. I felt helpless; I actually thought I was dead. A second RPG round was fired in our general direction, and it hit an old tree that had survived through the B-52 strike. The tree shook, and the branches fell. When I heard this, I realized then that I wasn't dead. I scrambled behind a two- to three-foot termite hill, into a small foxhole, and field dressed my wound. I was madder than hell that I'd been hit. I wanted to kill the bastards, but since I had lost my rifle, I had nothing to shoot back with." [26]

Ram-Jet says, "I found my way into the little foxhole. There were other people that were in the same hole or one next to it, about six or seven. They were on top of each other, all of them trying to gain cover by hiding behind the one skinny tree." [22]

Pat McCoy of the 1/2 says, "As the lead platoon of the company got to the top, we heard firing, and someone said over the radio to haul ass off the mountain so we just came back down. We heard that everything had been moved to Nui Ba Den. We understood that they had seen the one tunnel on the west side. We got to the base of Nui Cau about three thirty in the afternoon, and I remember that because we were trying to get muscle cramps out and find water and get some salt and that kind of stuff. That was when we heard on the radio that astronauts were taking off for the moon." [28]

Popcorn said, "I got my squad down from the mountain, all of them searching for cover after the firefight started. There was small-arms fire, RPGs, and AK-47s hitting the ground all around. I found my way to the already crowded foxhole occupied by my buddy Spike and others. I was the only one there who hadn't lost my rifle. Occasionally I saw puffs of smoke coming from the mountain or from the trees, and I opened up on them. My M-16 fire just drew more fire on them from the mountain and people yelled at me, 'Stop firing! You're going to get us hurt.'"[23]

Charlie Company Cdr. Capt. Howard was listening to the battalion net and heard news of the battle. He said, "I began to direct my company generally toward the mountain in case they were needed. They moved through elephant grass and a banana plantation."[25]

PFC Clarence Smith from First Platoon was wounded by the RPG. He was taken behind the trail, but he refused to be evacuated until he helped other wounded get back to the dustoff area.[22] SP4 John B. (Rocky) Rockafellow III was hit in the face by shrapnel, earning him his second Purple Heart. He and other members of First Platoon, Sgt. Bob Hall and SP4 Donovan (Spike) Kolness, and Third Platoon member SP4 David (Popcorn) Anderson tried to find cover in the tall elephant grass.[23] Second Platoon, who were the farthest up the mountain, deployed in a defensive position. Gilliam remembered looking down the mountain and seeing the men from First Platoon getting hit in the tall grass. He says, "They were trying to hide behind bushes and whatever they could find, but they had no place to hide."[24]

July 12 at 1:01 p.m.

Hall said, "I asked Spike to try to get my weapon, which was lying in the bomb crater. Popcorn tried to cover for him with his M-16, but it was to no avail. As Spike tried to retrieve the weapon, the NVA shot at him. Dirt began flying all over him. I yelled, 'Man, just get back here and leave it alone! There will be another one in a little bit.' We felt like toy ducks in a shooting gallery."[22]

Tennessee remembers, "Then they had us pinned down. I was firing back with the damn little ole M-79 grenade launcher that nobody wanted. The new guy got stuck with that. I was firing up at the mountain just to make noise. I never saw a soul that day."[16]

Charlie Company Cdr. Capt. Howard informed his platoon leaders via radio that an infantry company was in trouble on the slopes of the Black Virgin.[30]

Sgt. Tony Lombardi says, "We came racing up the road because my friend was in Alpha Company, Joe Zodda. The first thing I thought was, 'Oh my God, I hope Joey is not dead.' That's what I was worried about. I mean, Christ, we went to school together."(Joe Zodda was back in the rear.)[36]

Ram-Jet says, "All of the men felt helpless. Between us only one had a weapon and a few of us had lost their helmets. The M-16 that we did have was no good. Any time we fired it, we just drew more fire. The men remained in the foxhole for what seemed like minutes, but it was probably an hour or two, maybe three. When you're in a battle, all sense of time seems to go away."[23]

Alpha reported RPG and light firearm fire. Sgt. Gary (Wully) Wullenweber reported seeing a couple of NVA duck in and out of holes. Every once in a while, one would run over a boulder.[21] Gilliam remembered seeing the NVA pop up out of various holes, shoot, and then duck back into their tunnels[24]. SP5 Elmer R. Dehaven (Doc D) was Alpha Company's medic. Each platoon had a medic, and the company medic rode in his own track with the Headquarters section of the company. Doc D had been drafted and was a practicing Seventh-Day Adventist. He was classified as a conscientious objector, so they sent him to medic school. He and others lowered themselves into a punji pit and took cover.[11]

Ron Pilgrim said, "We felt like the stupidest sons-of-bitches in the world. Here we were up on a mountain with everybody shooting over the top of our rock. I like to shoot a lot, but that day there was nothing to shoot at. I mean, I never saw an enemy the entire day. We were trapped up there and we didn't want to get off. I'm glad we did get off before night came because they would have come in on us like hornets. You know, it's strange, but I don't know who the other two men were that were up there with me. One was a sergeant, but that's all I can remember about them. And the three of us got together and we spent a long time up there. We would look at each other and say, 'How the hell? We can't see anything. What the hell are we supposed to shoot at?'" [15]

Banks says, "All hell broke loose and we heard shouting, 'Get back off the mountain! Get back off the mountain!' We scattered, and I got separated from Lieutenant Williams." [19]

Phil says, "This Lieutenant Williams—we had some disagreements about ambushes and stuff. He sometimes, I think, was going to put us in danger. He'd say we'd go here, and I'd say, "No, we're not going there, sir. I said, 'This is where I'm going to be, and this is where I'm going to call the mortars.' I said, "You know, you want to court-martial me, fine. But I'm not going over there because you guys would never save my ass in time from there.' Well, he would just say some stupid things like, 'And are you going to do it.' I said, 'I'll see you in the morning, sir.'"

Phil continues, "The day before the battle, we actually went out on a dismounted mission, and he got us lost in the woods. You know what—I think we were actually in Cambodia. But there was a distinctive different terrain. We all felt it. I'm not kidding you. We thought, 'I don't know whether there was an imaginary border or what the shit it is, but there was something about it.' And we stopped and, you know what? I don't think our asses are supposed to be here, you know. And I'll tell you, sometime shortly after that happened ... we had to vamoose our asses out of there fairly quickly because we were in there and, all of a sudden—we were moving along, and then all of a sudden we came back and almost like doing 180 degrees and hurry your ass out of there. It was almost like we're in the wrong place."[20]

Banks continues, "I ended up with the first squad of the Third Platoon. I got in a bomb crater there with Ed and kind of covered while the others jumped in. It was the squad leader, Tom Pedigo, and about two or three others. We were firing up at the mountain, but we couldn't see what we were firing at or anything else."[19]

The battalion log stated, "1:10 - 21 Airborne for contact area. 2nd platoon is pinned down."[1]

Toney Mathews, the artillery Forward Observer, contacted the 4.2 mortars, who fired on the enemy positions. Mathews rejected the 81-millimeter mortars that Alpha Company had with them because he decided it would be hard to adjust them without risking friendly casualties. He was able to adjust fire for Alpha the entire afternoon without a single friendly casualty.

Toney also began using 105s and 155s from the Twenty-Fifth Infantry Division.[13]

1:15 p.m.—Issue 15 was on station and directed to report to Mathews. In the Twenty-Fifth Division, whenever there was any action, all airborne resources would come to the battle, and the FO or company commander would use any or all of them.[1]

1:30—Charlie Horse 35 (one light fire team) was on station. Meanwhile, Alpha Company Second/Thirty-Fourth Armor was ordered to support Alpha 2/2 (Mech). The tanks lined up on the road east of Alpha 2/2 (Mech).[1]

The tanks of A 2/34 began firing 90-millimeter HE rounds, but after thirty rounds, the firing from the NVA had not abated at all. Capt. Buckles began to adjust for them when he was near a radio. He would ask 2/6 to help spot.[7]

July 12 at 1:15 p.m.

"As the 90-millimeter tank rounds hit the boulders, they bounced off like ping-pong balls. They're having absolutely no effect," 2/6 observed, surprised.[7]

1:35—Yellow Jacket 005 was on station and was directed to report to FO Mathews.[1] Mathews's goal was to put a curtain of steel between the men of Alpha and the NVA; he continued to do this all afternoon.[13]

Mathews and Buckles met and decided that there was no reason to continue up the mountain. They decided it was almost suicidal to attack up a mountain when you could hardly see.[13]

1:45—Diamond Head 55 (one light fire team) on station.[1]

Chapter 13: APCs

Al Howard says, "Suddenly you could hear the AK-47s crackling, and then it all just started. I heard someone come over the intercom—you know, we had CVC helmets on—said, 'Get up to the base of the mountain and pick up the legs because they're getting cut down.'"[25]

Capt. Buckles radioed Second Platoon and said they were ordered to withdraw. Second Platoon met and decided how to withdraw with the least casualties.

2/6 briefed the Second Platoon, saying, "We'll go down the same way we came up. Spread out along the little berm. Put fire on the mountain so the First and Third Platoons can retreat. Now stay low and don't bunch up. We'll be okay if we don't present ourselves as targets." As the men executed my orders, I again reflected on how proud I was of the Second Platoon. At this point, they had taken no casualties. But in thirty minutes, except for a few individuals, the Second Platoon would cease to exist.[7]

Capt. Buckles got behind a boulder and yelled to the First and Third Platoons, "I realize we don't have the firepower to fight our way off the mountain!" So he ordered an immediate withdrawal. Bob recalls, "When we got to the mountain, we were as close as twenty yards from some of the NVA. I was standing right next to the captain. He had started up, and we had gotten five yards up the mountain. That's when everything opened up on us. We were just sitting ducks. We had people in front of and behind us; there were snipers in the trees." Capt. Buckles said, "I have called for some jets to bomb the mountain. We've got to get the hell off the base of the mountain. It's every man for himself!"[17]

July 12 at 1:31 p.m.

Popcorn says, "I noticed a man down about twenty-five yards from me. When I got up to go to Sgt. Maguire, he was pretty bad; Sgt. Maguire was almost dead if he wasn't dead already. I grabbed Maguire, and I tried to pull him toward safety. During this attempt, I was shot in the bottom of the foot. The bullet passed through the bottom of my foot, breaking many of the bones. When the bullet stopped, it stayed lodged in my foot, just under the skin on the top of my foot. More bullets from an AK-47 hit my helmet. They hit the curve of the helmet and the edge. The bullet hit the elastic band and ripped the canvas cover wide open. I didn't even realize how close I came to death until later. I had to drop Maguire and roll back into the grass for cover. Just then a sniper homed in on Maguire and shot him ... and shot him again and again. The sniper seemed to be trying to get a message across to the rest of us lying there in the open. The message was well taken. We thought we were gone for sure."[23]

Spike says, "S. Sgt. Harris lay out to our left with a severe wound to the arm near his elbow. He hollered and yelled due to the pain. We tried to calm him down. Popcorn tried to get his arm over to him and touch him and comfort him. Even that slight movement drew more fire. Harris's yells turned to more of a whimper, and he calmed down for a while. Then Harris let out a big yell because of the pain. That was probably when he was killed by a sniper. Harris was silent after that."[23]

Popcorn says, "I started reciting the Lord's Prayer, 'Our Father who art in Heaven ...' I was positive then that I would die that day. Spike joined in, 'Hallowed be Thy name.' We got about halfway through the prayer and neither of us could remember the rest. We believed that when we died, we were going to hell for not remembering. It literally scared the piss out of one of us"[23]

Tennessee recalls, "We took off across that grass field. We run like hell and headed back away from the mountain because we were all pinned down. I got wounded in the shoulder as I was leaving it. It was out there in the middle of that damned field where most of us got hit at."[32] Bob says, "I took off and ran as far as I could and then a sergeant grabbed me from behind and pulled me even further. I remember the sound of the shots hitting the elephant grass and seeing the grass being mowed down by the enemy fire."[17]

Pilgrim remembers, "It took us about an hour to get halfway up the mountain, but it only took five minutes to get back down. There were bullets all over. I mean, when we started going down off that mountain, there was no way you could protect yourself because you had to turn your back to the enemy. The worst, of course, was when we hit the bottom of the mountain where we had to go around these bomb craters. There was absolutely no cover, no grass left. It was just like hail coming down from above. We just ran as fast as we could. It was one open turkey shoot for those guys. My focus was on the tree line. I remember when I got across the open area and I found some rocks, and I dived over them. I remember the bullets splattering all around me, but I was safe behind this pile of rocks. I remember, my whole uniform—there wasn't a dry spot on it. And, you know, the strange part of that whole day was I had a canteen of water with me. This is how intense the whole battle was and how concentrated it was. I remember, to this day, I never took a drink of water the whole time I was up there on the mountain."[15]

2/6 says, "The NVA snipers looked for soldiers near a radio and tried to shoot them first. No one remembered any green tracers that day. The NVA unit may have been a specialized unit of snipers that didn't want to give their position away by firing tracers. The number of head shots seems to confirm this."[7]

Lee Stember took the M-60 and all of the 60 ammunition away from his trainee and threw them away, and the two scrambled down the mountain. "The kid that I was with kind of went into shock. He didn't know what to do. Well, first, I just threw the gun. I had my rifle and I was carrying 60 ammo. I took all that shit off and just kept my 16 ammo and my rifle. He never would have made it back carrying that big gun because, you know, he just couldn't. He was struggling. I got everything off him so he could run. I kept my M-16 and ammo, and we basically just got off the rocks. When we hit the bottom of the mountain, we would run about fifty feet and then just fall down and lay there until the fire let up a bit, and then we would get up and run again. That day was like none other that I can remember. I mean, I felt that my job was to get this new kid back alive, and I did that." [18]

Banks, Sgt. Tom Pedigo (who would receive his fourth Valor award in two months), and some other men jumped into a bomb crater near the base of the mountain and took cover. [19] Hall, Spike, and Popcorn went into a small depression at the base of the mountain. Firefight Williams was not with his RTO, and further contact with him was lost. [19] Toney Mathews and his RTO, Frank Lawrence, became separated. [13]

Mathews recalls, "I had gone around one side of this huge boulder and Capt. Buckles had gone the other way. Just when we saw each other, we began taking small-arms fire from AK-47s and RPGs. We gave up trying to find out if the caves held a cache of weapons or whatever in them. The fire started out light and then became heavier. Those of us on the mountain had some cover, while the poor soldiers at the base of the mountain were in the open. They began scrambling around looking for anything to hide behind. Shortly after, Buckles and I got separated. From what I understand, it was shortly after this that he was killed." [13]

Sgt. Freddie Daniels and SP4 Bernard J. Matthews, a man who got drafted when he let his student deferment run out, began to organize their platoon. Phil remembers, "When I think of Bernard Matthews, I remember the incident and the way his personality was. It was just, you know—he was kind of English, like, okay? He had a really quirky personality. I mean, his personality was good, but he had this bad habit. We'd be out there in the field, and drinking water is a very valuable commodity, okay? But he had to wash his hands and face all the time. And we'd just get so upset because he'd be washing his hands and face and then he just, he had to do it." When they realized that less than the entire platoon had made it out, they made plans to return.[20] Bernard Matthews would be killed July 28, 1969.[5]

Capt. Buckles's RTO, Ronald Cohen, told him that an RTO with others was lost at the base of the mountain and they needed help. Cohen was wounded soon after the conversation.[7]

July 12 at 1:47 p.m.

Someone came on the company net and told the drivers that they were needed at the base of the mountain. There was no one in charge of this unit, so the drivers began moving toward the mountain in the S&D formation with the command track, the commo track, and the medic track in the middle. Most of the drivers do not remember a call to come to the mountain. Hippie remembered that when the drivers heard the noise of battle, they started their engines and began moving toward the mountain of their own volition. They had heard over the radio, "They're everywhere! They're coming down the mountain, they're hiding behind boulders the size of houses, and they're coming out of caves. We need help!"[19] SP4 Arthur DiBattista started his engine and began the trip to the enemy's kill zone.[26]

SP4 Al Howard and the other line platoon drivers were heading for the base of the mountain.[25] SP4 Billy Benson, the driver for the captain's track, and Chris Freeze, the .50 gunner, began looking for a medevac area. When they found it, Van and Hippie brought the medic track forward to begin loading the wounded.[6] Forrest says, "I think the helicopters from the Twenty-Fifth would probably get the information about the battle from the Twenty-Fifth Infantry brigade commander, or whoever, possibly that general officer. He had an Air Force FAC (Forward Air Controller) with him.[34] "Al wrote in his diary that the drivers were told to stay back until after the jets had bombed the mountain.[25]

Al Howard says, "Then we took off to go back to the base. I don't recollect who was leading. We was just all on-line going up to the base of the mountain. We were heading for the place we dropped the legs off. We were just on-line more or less and just barreling ass up toward the mountain. Well, then there was a track to the right of me that ran into a bomb crater and turned over."[25]

Wully finally had a chance to look around. He noticed that men from other platoons had returned to the fight. After a quick search, Wully reported to 2/6 that there was an overturned track in a B-52 hole. Wully was given the assignment of extracting the men in the track. Wully pulled Hale, the driver, out but couldn't get SP4 Ron Rohden, the gunner, out of the hole. Hale climbed up to the lip of the crater and saw a track that had a shovel on the back. He grabbed it, returned to the overturned track, and began to dig out his gunner.

Wully saw the tracks come up from the rear position. One of the tracks, driven by PFC James Hale, fell into a B-52 crater.[21] SP4 James Nichols (a decorated soldier) was driving the track to the left of Hale. He maneuvered his track so that it was in front of the crater and provided some measure of protection for the men in the downed track. Jim Nichols and his .50 gunner, SP4 Larry, jumped off the track and tried to help the .50 gunner, Ron Rohden, who was pinned under the cupola and was complaining about his back. Two or three others also came to help.[26]

Larry said, "There was another guy just comes to my mind—I think we called him Hale. He had flipped a track in front of me. He flipped the track over in a bomb crater and, of course, when he did that, I had to get out, get the guys out of the track."[26]

Jim continues, "All I know is the .50 gunner was trapped, and I turned. I got the track up close enough to where the guys could get behind me away from small-arms fire, and I jumped out of the track to go back and help dig the .50 gunner out before he suffocated. You know that grass was high, and we were just barreling ass that way. I imagine he came up to that hole before he even knew it."

"When I got down to the hole, the driver was already out and he's hollering that his .50 gunner was trapped. Somebody said that there was so much equipment in there that they couldn't get to the gunner by the back door so we had to dig him out through the .50 cupola. We used our hands; it was kind of like sand in the bottom if it, the bomb crater, and we used our hands mostly."[26]

Other tracks got on line around the B-52 hole and tried to put down suppressive fire. In the past, when the tracks got on line and the .50 gunners, PFC Mike Benefield, SP4 Jimmy (Chief) Begay, SP4 Donald Paxton, PFC Fred Mathews, SP4 Sammy Labastida, and others, began firing, the enemy would duck their heads and the hard part of the battle would be over. That day, this maneuver didn't work. The enemy was too well concealed for the guns to have that effect. The firing from the mountain did slow down, though.[6]

Wully returned to 2/6 with Hale and Rohden, the two soldiers who had been in the overturned track. The gunner, Ron Rohden, was complaining about a bad back and was sent back to the rear.[21] Hale joined up with Wully's track and went back into the fighting to help find more wounded.[26]

Hall says, "Throughout all of this, Wully ran by and tried to help out as much as he could. Wully found a wounded soldier, his friend, one Colon-Coto, and carried him over to where we lay, hoping that it was a safe place to leave his friend. Colon-Coto was shot through the back of the leg, and the bullet came out of the bottom of his foot. He needed someplace safe to be. Colon-Coto couldn't walk, let alone run for cover. Wully tried to assess the situation and tried to make sure people had weapons and ammunition." Spike remembered this and said, "How Wully made it through all of this and didn't get shot is nothing short of a miracle."[22]

Second Platoon was the only platoon left on the mountain. They were using fire and maneuver to retreat in an orderly manner.[7]

Capt. Buckles grabbed Doc D and headed for Second Platoon. Doc D says, "The captain saw me and waved me over to him and said that we were going up the mountain to get some people. There was one other person that came with me, but I don't remember the other man's name. I know there was someone with me, but I didn't know who. Now that second time we went up, all hell broke loose. It happened twice, but that second time it was much worse."[11]

Mathews returned to the base of the mountain, and he saw S. Sgt. Cantor Hill. Hill had a LAW with him, the two of them decided where it would do the most good, and Hill fired. Both men moved to other positions. Mathews found that his RTO Frank Lawrence had been wounded. Toney Mathews took the radio and continued directing fire on the mountain. Mathews says, "I went and got across the field and dove behind a log. I was getting into position where I had some concealment and could still see the area the best I could. When I dove behind that log, I felt this tug and I thought, 'Well, I've been wounded.' I didn't feel any pain so I thought I was grazed or something. Later that evening when we were cleaning up our gear, I noticed that there was a hole from an AK-47 round that went through the flap of my canteen cover that I used to hold grenades. It couldn't have missed those grenades by more than a fraction of an inch." [13]

Toney Mathews and I had already started a friendship that would continue through the next forty-six years and to this day. I recall, "Toney impressed me with his intelligence and dedication to his role in Alpha Company. His ability to call in accurate artillery support had already earned Captain Comb's confidence. From the early morning Toney started plotting coordinates and giving them to the supporting artillery batteries. The batteries would follow our line of march and note areas where we would conduct reconnaissance missions. The last thing he would do at night was to plan and actually fire Def Con missions. Before concluding his planning, Captain Combs would contact all platoon leaders and tell them to get their men under cover. 'Lt. Mathews will now call in the very close artillery concentrations and he won't stop until I hear shrapnel hitting the tracks!'"

Some of the other platoon officers felt that being a West Point graduate made Toney aloof and stand-offish. But I appreciated his dedication to his craft. In a major fight,

Toney and his skills would create a wall of steel between Alpha and the enemy. Mathews would be the difference between life and death."[7]

Forrest remembers, "They would have a separate Div Arty (Division Artillery) net. They would be up on their own net. The artillery folk had the capability of talking to their direct fire support unit. I'm not sure which of their artillery units it was; in most cases, it would be their 105 unit. They had the capability of talking to us simultaneously without having to switch nets. Normally the air, after they received their initial information, would then switch to the Div Arty net or to the artillery net or the fire control net, is what it was called, simply because they would want to know what kind of artillery fire is going out so they could shut that off. Well, you're making me talk military here, and I haven't done that in a long time."

Forrest continued, "And that's normally the job of the FO. It does become personalized, if he's going to get indirect fire support from an Arty unit; I would not direct that. The operations officer would only verify friendly locations for him, or battalion artillery would have the battle plotted, but the actual placement of rounds and the actual placement of Air Force ordinance would be done by the FO on the ground. He would be the marker and the spotter and all those kinds of things. Now the way that I recall that was done is, when those fighters came on station, the first guy in with them was their airborne control. I'm trying to remember what they call those guys—but airborne FAC, he would talk directly to the FO. The FO would direct him to mark because he would fire from his OV10 Bronco.

"Those guys were on station first, and the communications between the FO and that airborne FAC was continual on a fire control net, not on a command net, because of all the traffic and the adjustments and the numbers that were necessary for them to do their fire. It was critical for them to stay on that net for two reasons—number one, to identify where friendly forces were, and to identify when artillery was incoming because they needed to get the hell out of there. There was always this question of coordination, of when to start one phase. One of the things that was really spooky was you had the indirect fire first and then you had the helicopter gunships and the AREA arrow rockets. Then the Air Force would come on board and—I may have it reversed. It may have been just the opposite, but somebody had to control all of that and normally it was at the battalion level. There was an FO at the battalion level who talked directly to FOs assigned to each of the companies."[34]

Chapter 14: Medevac Zone

S pike says, "Popcorn and I lay in the grass for a long while, until things calmed down. The APCs drove up, and we weren't sure if the APC drivers could see us. Being careful not to draw fire, we raised our arms and yelled until we were noticed. I got up and helped Popcorn to the rear of the APC. Popcorn hobbled over and hopped on the downed ramp at the back of the APC ... Ram-Jet and I and others picked up the body of Staff Sergeant Harris and loaded him onto the back of the track with the others. The APC then took us back to the medevac area so that Popcorn could be medevacked to safety."[22]

July 12 at 1:50 p.m.

Phil says, "Yeah, actually, the rice field was kind of dry. Because once the action started, the .50 gunners really poured it on, and then all of a sudden, somebody stopped them. They were still quite a ways back. They were quite a ways back 'cause I was worried about them shooting us because I thought, 'God, they're a long ways back there yet' and it was like they started to roll in and all of a sudden they just stopped. We ended up, finally, calling them; some of them started coming in because I started calling them in by hand action—just by moving my hand because I didn't have a radio. The radios were gone. There was nobody with a radio .We had no way to call for help or to know where the rest of the company was."[20]

Tennessee says, "As soon as the men on the tracks heard that there was wounded left in the grass, everyone in the outfit come in there to give us a hand. I don't know how long it took them to get to me. It might have been five minutes, it might have been five hours, and it seemed like two weeks. They come by and threw us on the back ramp of the tracks. They took us just like that." Tennessee remembers, "I was looking around, and it seemed like they had fifteen of us on that track. Some dead, some not. We were stacked like so much wood. They took us back like that. I could walk, so when we got back to the medevac area, I was one of the first to get on a helicopter."[32]

By two o'clock, Second Platoon was down at the base of the mountain with no casualties, but they did see wounded from other platoons who had been abandoned and were treating them. Capt. Buckles and Doc D arrived and told 2/6 that there was an RTO left on the mountain. After a short argument, Capt. Buckles and the medic headed toward the mountain.

2/6 joined Capt. Buckles and Doc D as the three of them dove into a bomb crater at the base of the mountain. Capt. Buckles looked over the rim of the crater to see if he could find the RTO, and he was hit by a bullet right between the eyes.[45] He slumped over, and Doc D cradled him in his arms, but Capt. Buckles was dead. 2/6 ordered Doc D to go to the base of the mountain and get S. Sgt. Hill to bring up a team to extract Capt. Buckles. 2/6 got wounded for the first time.[7]

Doc D says, "Once the captain got hit and the lieutenant was hit, why, I had to get up and run back to find a sergeant. I found a sergeant and told him to get a track up so we could load the captain's body on it, but when he turned around to leave, bless his heart, he was hit. Then as a last recourse I ran back to the radioman, and as soon as I got there, he too was hit. He did radio back, and eventually the track came and we got the old man's body off the battlefield. Evidently, that's when we got out. I don't remember."[11]

Even though he was wearing one of the new thirty-pound flak jackets, Firefight was hit in the chest. He was taken to the rear to be evacuated.[6] Gilliam was hit in the leg and began crawling back to find the medic track.[24] Sgt. Jerry Campbell and S. Sgt. Philip Deering began to organize their squads to return to the battle, where they began extracting wounded.[33]

Phil remembers, "My driver was looking for directions; he was looking anyway. So they come in closer to us so we can move and stuff like that. They were actually being shot. Yeah, and then they started coming around, turning around because you couldn't shoot at anything and the guys were in front of you and these big rocks and you couldn't look over them."[20]

Jerry said, "It was dumb. I remember the guys talking about it. What the hell did those goddamn bombs do? It didn't do shit here, you know. There are big holes out there in the ground we've got to get around all the time. They were solid, just huge boulders. Right. I don't know if anybody saw a single enemy."[33]

Phil continues, "The shot that wounded me went down through the leg. It came down—it was a real sharp angle. I was trying to help get some of these wounded guys out of there is what happened. The shot was more like a seventy-five-degree angle there. It only went down probably just a half inch. I tell you what. I fell. I mean, as soon as I was hit, I fell. I was angry. Yeah, I was angry, and then the trouble is—what I was trying to do was get these other guys out of there, and then all of a sudden, I couldn't move my leg. At first, I didn't think I could move my leg. I thought—I looked at it, you know, there was blood and everything, and I thought it was bad, really bad. I thought, 'Oh, shit.' So then I moved my leg 'cause it was kind of like a burning sensation—then 'I can walk fine,' so then I just got up and started helping the other guy. We had this guy there that was just really bad off. He was screaming and yelling."[20]

Throughout all of this, Hall and Ram-Jet remained pinned down in the little foxhole until the APCs could come and get them. The first to reach them was Wully, who told Hall that he was going to take him back to the tracks and that the tracks were well on their way. Wully asked Hall, "Can you make it to the wood line with that hole in your leg?" Hall looked at him and said, "I guarantee you that even with the shrapnel in my leg, I will run over you if you get in the way." Hall remembers, "I ran across the field to try to get to safety. As I ran through the bombed-out area, we were being shot at from three directions. We made it to the tall grass and went down for some cover. I popped a smoke grenade to help the APCs find me. Soon I saw a track coming directly for me. Of all the tracks to get there, it was my own."[22]

July 12 at 2:00 p.m.

Hall says, "I got on my track, and there was an M-60 and some belted ammunition. Since I didn't have my rifle or a helmet, I grabbed the M-60 and found a helmet. The track headed back toward the base of the mountain. Ram-Jet and others helped us to load bodies onto the track. We weren't sure if these bodies were alive or dead; we didn't have time to check."[22]

Jim says, "After we got the gunner out, we started helping wherever we could. We was giving them cover with the APCs. I moved up front to retrieve the legs that walked up the mountain, and we all started retrieving back. We were still getting small-arms fire and stuff like that as we retrieved back. After we got back a safe distance. [The officers] started calling in the air strikes and dropping Willy Pete all over the mountain. I don't remember much other than taking orders from my platoon sergeant, Sgt. Wullenweber. He would tell us to do something, and then he would take off and do something else."[26]

Jerry says, "I left the mountain and found a bomb crater, but I didn't stay in it. Hell, I just hit. I made it this far, so I went out on the other side. I didn't stay there long at all. I just dove in it to get away and then, well, I gave a little prayer, got up on the other side, and started running. Then I got out there in the middle of the grass where I could see a little bit what's going on. I could see my track and I ran to that."[33]

Second Platoon extraction team of Doc D, Cantor Hill, Wully, Johnny King, and Tribble arrived. 2/6 and Tribble provided cover while the others hauled the body of Capt. Buckles off the mountain. Once at the base of the mountain, the body was given to SP4 Leonard (Wayne) Compton, SP4 Dennis Laken, and PFC Johnny King. Johnny King was a nineteen-year-old soldier from Sanford, North Carolina.[50] He had been in country just two months and yet, after carrying Capt. Buckles's body to the rear, Johnny and the others returned to the battle. Once he got there, Johnny was shot in the head and died.[50]

Sgt. Hall remembers, "My men loaded fifteen to twenty dead and wounded onto the back of the track, and then we went to the medevac area. As soon as we offloaded the wounded, we went back to the base of the mountain. I knew where the first RPG shot came from, so I opened up on the area and kept steadily pumping lead into the area until I melted the barrel of the M-60."[22]

Hall continues, "Even though I was one of the first to be hit, I was one of the last to be dusted off. I could have gotten off earlier, but I worried about my buddies. Those people were as close to being brothers to me as my own brothers."[22]

July12 at 2:06 p.m.

2/6's RTO, Bob Oerther, was hit in the butt. The bullet had gone in one cheek and out the other. SP4 Daniel King picked him up and carried him back to the medevac area.[7] Sgt. Calvin Maguire was killed by a bullet in the head. Sgt. Calvin Harris, a twenty-three-year-old man from Rosedale, Louisiana, was hit in the back and died. He lay near the bottom of the mountain and was hit numerous times after his death.[57] SP4 Alberto (a crazy Puerto Rican), nicknamed Colon-Coto, was hit in the thigh, and the bullet went out the bottom of his foot.[14] Medic England had patched up Colon-Coto and was seeing to other wounded. S. Sgt. Hill was wounded and carried to the medic track by Sgt. Richard Karpinski. When Doc England finally got to Johnny King, he himself was killed by a shot to the head.[47]

Doc D says, "I was caring for Richard England. That boy wasn't in country no time. God love him. He was young and brand new, and he didn't even know what it was all about yet. He never lived long enough to learn."[11]

Danny King said, "I let this guy get killed. He was a black man, his eyes were as big as saucers, and he was yelling, 'Help me! Help me!' He had been hit, but not that bad. I said, 'Get down! Get down!' He didn't do what I said. He didn't get down, and he got hit again. Why didn't I just pull him down? Why didn't I just reach over and pull him down? He was only about three feet away."[27]

Daniel Waggenaar, a twenty-year-old from Richland, Washington, who had been in country four months, was killed by a shot to his head. Dan was blonde and six-foot-plus tall with a stocky, Swedish build. In the evenings, he would read his Bible, but in a battle he was a terror. He was considered one of the best .50 gunners in the company. We are not sure why he was on the ground that day. Phil says, "Dan Waggenaar didn't drink, he didn't smoke, he stayed away from the whores, but you know what? He was the best machine gunner I ever had in my life. When we used to get into a fight, I'd have to yell at him to get down. Every night he'd go back and read his Bible. He was the most religious guy in my squad as well as the best machine gunner I had ever known. I couldn't keep him down."[20] Wully began guarding him.

George Kimmel, a twenty-one-year-old from Cumberland, Maryland, was shot in the head and died immediately.[49] Sgt. Steven Cummins, a twenty-year-old soldier from Eau Gallie, Florida, who had completed Noncommissioned Officers Candidate School (NCOCS), carried George Kimmel's body back to the medic track, loaded him, and then headed back to the mountain, where he was killed[46]. Steve had been in country since May 12. The medic track took ten or twelve bodies back to the medevac area, and it is probable that during this trip, Kimmel's body fell off the track and was lost in the elephant grass.[14]

Forrest says, "One of the biggest nightmares that I had as a result of the big fight in '65 is that we lost a kid. We had a kid named John Ackeson who was wounded in November of 1965—was reported to have been medevacked out of the battle site on about the seventeenth or eighteenth of November. I got a letter from his mother in December that said she had not heard from him since November. Now, we started to check, and again, when folks say, "Well, he was medevacked with the rest of the guys," we assumed in all the chaos that that is, in fact, what happened. Well, we chased the hospital pipeline and couldn't find him. Went back to the Ia Drang Valley in April of the following year and found his boots with dog tags where he had been left out there. Now, I don't know whether he was dead when we left him or what, but he was left behind."[34]

Jerry recalls, "Then I went and found Sgt. First Class Johnson and picked him up. We turned the track around and went straight forward. We picked up a couple guys, but Johnson, I remember, because I was going to go home before he was—not that much, but a month or whatever, and he said, 'Jerry, I'm going to beat you home.' And I said, 'Well, as long as you get home.'"[33]

Pilgrim remembered, "I was so relieved at being alive that I lit up a cigarette and took a long swig of that warm water, and to this day that was the best-tasting cigarette and drink of water in my entire life. I stayed there for about twenty minutes, said a prayer of thanks, and then a guy came up to me and told me that there were wounded on the field of battle, so I guess we started pulling wounded guys out. We did that right to the end of the day."[15]

"We were pulling this wounded guy out, myself and this other guy, and I think I had his head and shoulders and the other guy was holding his feet. We were just back at the corner of an APC when all of a sudden the guy got his knee shot out, and he drops that end. The round intended for me bounced off the APC, and half of it went into my arm and half went into my leg. It kind of knocked me down, but I could still hobble around."[15]

Tennessee was put aboard the medic track and remembered being stacked like wood—some wounded, some dead. Colon-Coto, S. Sgt. Steve Friend, SP4 Charles Roberts, and SP4 Dominic Cuizio were among the wounded; Capt. Buckles was among the dead. Wully had carried Colon-Coto back to the track, and Hippie remembered trying to bandage him up. Colon-Coto was in extreme pain. Hippie remembered seeing large chicom grenades in the trees, but the wires weren't connected, probably because of the Arc Light Strike the night before.[14]

Doc D made it back to the medevac area and began to tend to the wounded. He was amazed at the bravery of the helicopter pilots and gunners. He stated, "Many a man on the choppers jumped off and gave us a hand. I didn't fix anybody until I got back to the dustoff area. I don't have any idea how many people I worked on that day. We were trying to get them into the choppers as fast as we could. It was just that the wounded were everywhere. Soldiers

July 12 at 2:18 p.m. would come up and drop off a wounded man and then just turn around and go back to the battle. There was no one around to give any orders; everyone just did what he had to. Everyone was a hero that day. God love them—they did their jobs. I didn't see anybody panic; all I saw were heroes everywhere."[11]

Van says, "Our company medic, Doc D, [was] the best medic that I ever saw while I was over there. You know the thing that I remember best about Doc D is that his hair was always in place. He could walk all day through the jungle and when he took his helmet off not a hair would be out of place."[14]

Forrest says, "As soon as the soldiers heard there were wounded back up there, in groups of two or three, they made their way back to help their buddies. I had been with some good units but 2/2 was an absolutely superb fighting unit. I know that guys like Kelly and some of those other guys on the Thunder Road and in the rubber at An Loc and Quan Loi—these guys were tigers. That's what I think more of these books need; this is the stuff that they need to write about."[34]

Sammy Labastida says, "I don't know what happened. As things went on, everything just got really confusing, and I think a lot of people were scared. I was scared. You know, I didn't know what to do, and communications was poor. The drivers only went so far, then we had to stay. Then all hell broke loose, and I think we tried to make sure that all of us in the First Platoon were going to be close to each other.[26]

"Al was helping me with the fight. He was exposing himself to enemy fire by pouring oil on the barrel of the .50 while I was shooting at the NVA. I ran through three barrels on the machine gun, and he helped me replace them. I guess Al and I were lucky. Once we got to the mountain, we didn't have any cover. All we could do is just take it. We didn't get hit, but I know we had some men in the track that had been wounded. I guess we brought back two or three wounded men. I don't know how we decided it was time to go back or what, but then we started heading back."[26]

Phil says, "There was a black guy that I helped, and I was a little more pinned down than I really wanted to be. He was just ahead of me, and he kept getting hit in the leg. I think he lost his leg is what he did. All I know is that he must have got hit about four or five times in the same leg, 'cause I finally got up enough close enough to try to tell him to calm down. He kept moving every time he got hit. Well, obviously, you do, but there he was just like a sitting duck and every time I'd try to get a foot closer, the same thing would almost happen to me and I kept crawling closer. Finally, one of the tracks finally came up ahead and I was able to direct them to get in front of me, in the front of him, and then we got behind the track. I told them to lower the gate down and I picked the wounded up and put them on back of the gate."[20]

Don Weber's memory of that day is seared in his mind, but his memory is of a very condensed part of the battle. Don was the .50 gunner on 2/6's track. This was the track that most of the orders came from, so with no officer or NCOs present, Don took over communicating to the other three tracks of the Second Platoon.[26]

Don remembers the general. He says, "I didn't hear what was said, but the word went through the company like wildfire. Before we went up that hill, everybody knew the general sent us up. It wasn't something we heard afterward. It was something we knew before. Most everybody knew right out front that we were going to be in trouble if we did that. We heard enough about the mountain. The story I heard was that it was [at] one time a volcano, that it had numerous tunnels running through it. We heard that the main fortified area was in the rock slide because it provided so much cover. That was the main reason we didn't want to assault that part of the mountain.[26]

"So once the firing started, what I remember was we put the tracks on line. We moved up to a position where we could cover the mountain but far enough away so we had a good angle of fire. We were firing up the mountain so that we wouldn't hit our own people. We wanted a clear separation of fire between the .50s and our own men.[26]

"Our people had been coming off the mountain for some time. The gunners were firing at the mountain, and the drivers, of course, were sitting tight, doing what they normally do and trying to be invisible. Anyway, the command came over the radio that Second Platoon was to come forward and then hold until all of the other tracks had pulled off, and then pull your men off."[26]

"What I remember is, as the platoon to my left pulled off, more rounds started coming in at me. I don't remember any RPGs then, but I distinctly remember small arms and machine gun fire coming at our group. I was firing at an area on the mountain that had a big cloud of smoke on it. I figured something had happened there so I was firing at it. I realized that almost everybody was gone from the base of the mountain, and I started to feel the adrenaline really pumping.[26]

"Then there were four tracks left, and I called off one track at a time. First one, then another, and I'd watch out of the corner of my eye. They'd pull back and swing and take off, and each time they did that, the noise of the rounds coming by and pinging around me would intensify. I finally pulled the last track other than mine, and I was champing at the bit to go. And as soon as it turned around and started pulling off, I had the driver turn around, and the fire was really intense. I heard and felt as much as I heard the ring of a round that hit the back of my cupola. I feel, in my mind, fortunate that I always rode with the cover up because that round would have gone through the back of my neck if I didn't have my cover up. The bullet did spray the inside of the cupola. It shredded my book that I was reading, and it threw little bits of spray into my arm.

"I picked up that paperback after the battle, and it was full of holes. The force of the bullet kept coming around, went through my book, and I got some in the arm. That was my big WIA. They asked me if I wanted a Purple Heart for it, but I said, 'You got to be kidding me.'"[26]

Banks says, "We finally managed to get back to where the mortar platoon lieutenant was. He was on top of his track, and we [were] so hot. It is like 115 degrees, and the jungle and carrying the radio and trying to fire back and everything, I was feeling heat exhaustion."[19]

PFC Banks says, "Suddenly we realized that, somehow or another, NVA were down there at the bottom of the mountain too. They weren't just on the mountain; they were in the jungle behind our troops. I got some guys together—one had an M-79—and we went into the trees and began firing. I saw more than one fall out of the palm trees. The NVA had snipers in those trees. We were surrounded; they were everywhere because they shot down a medevac chopper that was coming in from behind. We went back into the trees and continued firing until there was no more firing coming back from there."[19]

Banks continues, "I remember a man named Ken. How he got on a dustoff chopper and got gone, I don't know. He was back a couple of days later. They found him at the hospital at Cu Chi, but what he was doing there, I don't know. He wasn't wounded or anything. He just got on one of those choppers and was gone. We don't know if he went with a buddy or what. I couldn't blame him really for leaving; things were really bad that day."[19]

Doc D says, "Our dustoff area was close enough to the battle to be in danger. We were trying to get the wounded on the choppers while we were taking fire from the trees.

Some of the crew of the choppers would jump off and help me carry guys 'cause we were really beat. We were all done in." A chopper was shot down as it was trying to land. Fortunately no one in the battalion was hurt. That one was later taken off the field of battle by a flying crane.

Bob remembers, "I got back to where the tracks were as it was safer there than being in the open. I was hiding behind a track, and a shell went off the side of the metal and threw shrapnel into my neck. The wound didn't knock me out of action. I was told to help this soldier get the captain into the helicopter."[17]

Wully saw booby traps and electrically detonated grenades lying on the ground.[21] Sgt. First Class Steward was hit in the arm, and SP5 Mike Mirenda untied his bootlaces and made a tourniquet.[12] Later, Jerry Campbell would find SFC Steward and evacuate him to the medevac area. Chief was hit, but after first aid, he refused to be evacuated and stayed with his company.[20]

July 12 at 2:30 p.m.

At two thirty, the battalion log reads, "A 2/2 still in heavy contact. A Co Commander wounded. 1st Platoon still pinned down."[1]

Medic PFC Robert Sires had patched up PFC Robert Childers and PFC Rickie Walker when he noticed that SP4 Phillip Beck was wounded. With SP4 Francisco Cruz providing cover fire, Robert Sires, a twenty-year-old from Spring Grove, Minnesota, tried to patch him up and was killed for his effort. Sires had been in Vietnam less than a month.[52]

Danny King said, "I ran. There was no cover. I see this little clump of grass, so I dive behind it. There is already a guy there. I'm lying right on top of him, and he gets hit and I don't. He got hit in the foot, and I'm lying there right on top of him. Bigger, smarter, faster, better-looking guys are getting hit, getting killed all around me. How come I didn't even get hit? His name was David Anderson. We called him Popcorn 'cause his hair was as white as popcorn, looked like popcorn."[27]

Hippie says, "Danny King was an Indian. He was pretty 'gung-ho.' I remember him as a great warrior. The funny thing about King was that he always looked like he was ready for inspection. His uniforms were always clean and pressed, and his boots were shined. He always had a fresh haircut. I never figured out how he stayed that way."[14]

The PFCs and SP4 finally made it back to the medic track. The heat that day was estimated to be somewhere from 110 to 120 degrees Fahrenheit. Banks had heat exhaustion, and part of the day is a blur for him. Many others also reported that the heat had gotten to them that day. SP4 Ron Pilgrim, Sgt. Ed Hennes, and the other soldier on the mountain finally made a dash to get off of it. They made it to the base of the mountain, ran across the grassy area, and found some rocks. After a cigarette and a drink, Ron returned to help find wounded men.[15]

After this horrendous battle, Popcorn remembers that he and Hall ended up on the same helicopter taking them to the hospital at Tay Ninh. Popcorn says, "I remember watching the medics remove the bullet from the top of my foot and handing it to me. I still have that bullet to this day."[23]

July 12 at 2:40 p.m.

2/6 called Lt. Mulhern on the radio and informed him of the situation. He strongly suggested that Mulhern bring the APCs forward. Mulhern was apprehensive about bringing the mortar tracks forward, as a single hit with an RPG would cause an explosion that could hurt many troops. When he was informed that Capt. Buckles had been killed, he ordered his men to the battle. 2/6 was then wounded for the second time, in the arm.[8]

Mulhern brought the mortar tracks to the area and saw Capt. Buckles's track. He dismounted his own track and got on the radios on the company and battalion nets.[8]

Tennessee continues, "They took us to some little MASH-type hospital. The place was full when I got there. There had been another firefight someplace else. They finally looked at my wound and seen that I had been hit straight through the shoulder, so they put a bandage on me and gave me some pain medicine and set me in a corner with my arm in a sling."[32] Streightiff got back to the medevac area.[17]

Nichols slowly backed his track toward the medevac area. Some of the men used his track to get off the mountain and carry a wounded soldier.[26] The tankers called Mulhern, and by using the track drivers as spotters, he was able to adjust fire.[8]

2/6 called Mulhern and said that they needed immediate help. Mulhern stood on top of his track but couldn't see anything, so he had the .50 gunners fire straight ahead.[8]

July 12
2:52 p.m.

PFC Dennis Brown, a driver for Alpha, was driving at the base of the mountain when an enemy round started his smoke grenades in the track on fire. He immediately threw them out the back of the track and was burned in the process.[56] He was later dusted off to Cu Chi with PFC Charles Gunn and SP4 Robert Dayton.

S. Sgt. Phillips Deering, who would get his second Silver Star and his second Purple Heart, was wounded while helping other wounded. He stayed near the battle site and wasn't dusted off until July 13, 1969.[20] SFC Vernon Johnson was wounded in the stomach while helping other wounded men. PFC William Gillespie was hit by shrapnel in the left arm, but he refused treatment to help recover wounded. He was dusted off after helping many men back to the dustoff area. Sgt. Bob Hall was a squad leader that day who already had one Purple Heart. He was wounded, but when his .60 gunner was hit, he manned the machine gun and stayed with it until the track withdrew to the medevac area.[22]

PFC Dennis Jones was an M-16 gunner that day. He stayed on after being wounded in the left leg. SP4 Keven Keleher was the Third Platoon medic. He stayed near the base of the mountain treating many wounded until he was hit himself. SP4 Ron Pilgrim picked up his third Purple Heart that day. Van and Hippie heard him hollering in the grass to come and get him.[57]

SP4 Terry Shaw was a driver who made repeated trips to the base of the mountain before he was hit and evacuated. PFC Robert Tribble provided covering fire while Capt. Buckles's body was being removed. He and 2/6 were the last two Alpha soldiers on the mountain. Tribble was later wounded. SP4 (Gomer) Wallace was wounded while providing cover fire with his .50-caliber machine gun.[57]

C 2/2 got an order to reinforce Alpha, and they left immediately. They traveled through the bush and then along a road. There was a report that, because of the danger of mines, a team was dismounted to act as mine sweepers.[29]

July 12 at 3:00 p.m.

The battalion log reads, "A 2/2 needs urgent dustoffs. Estimated twenty WIA, two KIA at this time."[1] Mulhern told 2/6 that dustoffs were already taking place for Cu Chi and that Charlie Company was coming in to reinforce them. Doc D remembered that there was no one around to give orders, but men kept coming from the battle site with their wounded comrades, and after they put them down, the men went right back into the battle. Doc D says, "I think that Alpha was full of heroes that day."[11]

Men from other platoons had fought their way back to the base of the mountain and were taking direction from 2/6. All of the senior NCOs had been hit by that time, Capt. Buckles was dead, and Lt. Williams was out of the picture. This left only Lt. Ladensack, Lt. Mathews, Lt. Mulhern, Sgt. Wully, and S. Sgt. Deering to organize the remainder of the company. The fire from the mountain had begun to abate.[7]

Gilliam found Nichols and told him that there were wounded at the base of the mountain. They took the track and tried to find the men, but someone had already evacuated them. They did find three other wounded on the field and put them on the track. Gilliam says, "After I rested up a little bit there, I went back out there to find my buddies, and I never did see them guys again, so evidently somebody got them. Everything was so screwed up that day that people didn't know what to do. It was chaos. The tracks just took off, and there wasn't anyone with any authority around. Everybody just done it—done what they had to do, trying to help other people."[24]

During one of their many trips to the mountain, Van and Hippie were extracting wounded and finding stretchers from other tracks. As they were ready to depart, the .50 machine gun was hit by a bullet and stopped firing. Hippie was hit in the hand by shrapnel and ducked inside the track to inform Van, but Van hollered, "You aren't bleeding! Get back up there!" A bullet then entered the track right beside Van's head and bounced around the inside of the track until it was spent. Hippie grabbed an M-16 and continued firing.[14] I came over to the medic track and shouted, "Quit fucking around! Get out of shot range!"[7]

Around three thirty, Pat McCoy of B 1/2 was at the base of Nui Cau, on the northwest side. He was trying to get the muscle cramps out and find water and salt when he heard over a radio that the United States had launched the mission to the moon. B 1/2 was told to go to Buell for the night.

Pat continues, "After resting, our company began to walk south to Fire Support Base Buell, where we spent the night. We knew that there was a big battle on the east side of the mountain because you could see air coming in, you could see the helicopters coming back and forth, and the word was going around what was happening was they tried to send tracks up the bottom of the mountain, from the bottom up, and they just got slaughtered. When we found out that they had dismounted and gone up without the tracks, we thought that it sounded really dumb. I mean, they weren't like grunts."[28]

July 12 at 3:30 p.m.

Vinson called Mulhern to get a sit-rep (Situation Report). Mulhern gave a body count and stated that there was an overturned vehicle in a bomb crater. Mulhern requested urgent reinforcements.[8]

2/6 (me) and Mathews met at the base of the mountain, and we decided that even though Toney was senior to me, I should keep command of the company. Toney knew Artillery, and that was where to best use his talents.[7]

Chapter 15: HQ Reaction

At four thirty, Lt. Col. Vinson and Command Sgt. Maj. Knox arrived at the medevac site. Vinson stayed there while Knox went forward to assess the situation.[41]

Phil recalls, "I remember Lt. Ladensack 'cause I remember running up to him and saying, 'Look, guys.' He was hit; I was hit in the leg. He was hobbling, and I was hobbling. And I say, 'Look, I got to have a track anyway. We've got some guys up there I've got to get out of there,' so I remember that. You know, all I remember is that he was talking on the radio. He was the guy that had a radio and he was talking on it, so he's got to be talking to somebody. I said, 'I just needed some communication to get something going.' There a twist to that story. Now I understand why—now I can kind of understand why it was so damn easy for them to be picking guys off. Jesus Christ! 'Cause we did. We lost, well, like you said—Christ, all the officers were gone, just like that, in a flash."[20]

Phil says, "I guided the track up. The driver totally dropped his gate; I put two guys on and maybe three guys. And we went on back that way, back to the medevac area, loaded them up there. Then I went back. Oh, then, Doc grabbed a hold of me someplace along that medevac line. Yeah, he saw my leg, and he says, 'I've got to take care of that. You've got to get on the —' I say, 'No, just wrap it up. I don't think it's that bad.' So he took a look at it, he wrapped it up, he says, 'You've got to get on the helicopter.' I say, 'I can't. There's nobody left.' And I said, 'Somebody has to help these men. Organize this.' I've got guys out there and so I was heading back out there. At that point, pretty much everybody stopped shooting and was walking or wounded, and then we started pulling back. We ended up about five hundred yards from where we were fighting."[20]

In the early evening, Hippie talked to Doc D about the day. Doc D was dazed and said that it was just terrible up there, but he was amazed at the bravery of the troops. He said that nobody had a chance to make it out, and he couldn't believe that anyone had made it back. Ron Rohden was in pain and sitting next to the medic track. Hippie saw a target and opened up. The spent cartridges went down the back of Ron's shirt and burned him.[14]

Van mentions that he doesn't remember taking a drink of water that day. Only Pilgrim remembered drinking. Both Van and Wully stated that there just wasn't time to take a drink. There was too much happening.[14]

SP4 Don Weber, the .50 gunner on Second Platoon Command track, called each track from Second Platoon to the rear to provide support for the helicopters.[26] Only the command track remained when 2/6 made one final search and found Mathews in a small bomb crater talking on the radio. Mathews had been calling in artillery and air strikes all afternoon.[7]

July 12 at 4:40 p.m.

2/6 remembers, "Throughout the battle I kept looking for Toney Mathews. I couldn't find him, and when I asked soldiers if they had seen him most said no. One said that he thought Toney had been shot. I conducted a fast sweep of the battlefield before I retreaded and found Toney in a small hole behind the berm. He had his radio with him and was shooting his M-16 at the mountain. I dove down beside him, and he said, 'I've seen those little rascals pop up behind the boulder, and I think I've hit a couple.' I told Toney to pick up his radio and follow me. He responded that he was directing the artillery and air strikes and that he could not leave. 'We are the last two people left on the battlefield,' I pleaded. Toney immediately picked up his radio, hopped up, and said, 'Let's go!'"[7]

2/6 remembers, "I began to ground guide my track back to the dustoff area. Weber was hit in the arm by shrapnel, and fragments hit me, wounding me for the third time that day. Don Weber was a soldier that wore a peace sign on his chest, but even though he was slightly wounded, he refused a Purple Heart. A soldier named Ken loaded one of his wounded buddies aboard a helicopter and then jumped on board with him. He was found two days later at the Cu Chi Hospital. He had not been wounded himself."[7]

Bob says, "I was told to help this soldier get the captain into the helicopter. Finally someone told me that I was to go on the next chopper. I got on, and we landed shortly in the hospital at Cu Chi. I got treatment for my wound, got some fluids in me, and they sent me back to my company before the day was over."[17]

Gilliam says, "I got to the hospital and I had to wait, you know. The very serious ones, they took them first. Then they put a bandage on my leg; I could still walk and everything. All they done was cleaned the wound and bandaged it because it wasn't all that serious as some of them. Then the next day, they sent me back to my outfit. It was slimmed down, you know—they're several that got killed and they was a bunch of them wounded. It was like me and three other guys standing there and when it was over, I was standing there by myself. It was like three to one killed or wounded. I don't know—I was just lucky, I reckon. I had to be, didn't I?"[24]

Command Sgt. Maj. Knox found 2/6 treating the wounded gunner and said, "You look like you need a hand, Lieutenant." Command Sgt. Maj. Knox was followed by Charlie Company. One of the helicopters was shot down and crash-landed close to the tanks and behind Lt. Col. Vinson. It remained there all night. The mountain was covered with smoke from the smoke grenades, bombs, and ammunition being used.[7]

The battalion log says, "4:50 - Dusted off so far = 17 litter 6 amb."[1] One of the things most of the men remember is the huge number of helicopters that were in the air that day.

Pilgrim added, "I don't remember a lot from the time I got hit until I went out on the last chopper. At least I was told it was the last chopper. I don't know if I waited there a while to get on the last chopper because I wasn't hit as bad or what. I remember when I got on the chopper there were rounds going through it. There were a lot of people on that chopper. I'm sure that it was overloaded. There were people laying on top of me, and that was fine 'cause I felt safer underneath them. There were still a lot of rounds going through the chopper before we got away."[15]

July 12 at 4:50 p.m. The battalion log reads, "5:00 p.m. - A 2/2 moving north to establish FOB (Forward Operating Base) with A 2/34 & C 2/2."[1] 2/6 found Capt. Howard, the commander of Charlie Company, and briefed him and his officers on the situation. They were advised that there were casualties lying in the grass near the base of the mountain. [29]

Capt. Howard remembers, "When I first got there, Alpha Company was in absolute disarray. They had already started to bring in helicopters; they were Twenty-Fifth Division ships, but I clearly, to this day, remember a radio transmission that said, 'This is—whatever his number was—we can't get in to pick anybody up because it's too hot.' And about that time over the same net came, 'This is Little Bear,' and some call sign. I don't remember the numbers, but Little Bear was a Log Bird from the Twenty-Fifth Division. 'This is Little Bear 123. I'm on my way out with my third load of wounded. I'll be back for more. *Out!*' And he came back in and, unfortunately, either on his next run or the one after, he took a hit in the hydraulic line but safely autorotated or made a running landing in the vicinity."[29]

Wullenweber and four or five other members of Alpha met up with Capt. Howard, and they began to look for more wounded.[21] Charlie drove their tracks through the rice paddies, and many of the men were dismounted and getting filthy. About one hundred meters from the mountain, Charlie was told that the dead and wounded were about halfway between them and the mountain. [20]

Charlie Company got on line, began to fire with all of their weapons, and started to look for additional wounded. Capt. Howard and his FO, 2nd Lt. Charles Horner, began to call in mortars and artillery and to adjust fire from the tanks. They also had some Cobra gunships at their disposal.[29] Sgt. Tony Lombardi noticed that the NVA were coming out of holes on the mountain, firing, and then going back into their lairs.[36]

July 12 at 5:02 p.m. Capt. Howard adds, "And when I first got there, we pulled in right near our Alpha Company to assess the situation. I saw that everything was in disarray, but they were trying to establish security to get the wounded in and out. I was trying to get an assessment of where Alpha Company stood and what we could do to get everybody out of there, who was in charge, and so forth. I made my way over to a group of soldiers. I asked, 'Who's in charge?' I said, 'Where's the company commander?' The first response I got was from some private, who was kind of lying on the ground behind a tree, and he was crying and he said, 'He's dead.' I said, 'I know that.' I had already heard over the radio that Dick Buckles was killed, and I knew that a lot of others had been hit, so I said, 'I know that, but who's in command?' And they said, 'The lieutenant' and pointed to Lt. Ladensack."

Capt. Howard continues, "Yes, across the way to this open field. He had been wounded; I believe he had been hit in the arm, and he was behind his track. And he was trying to get everything under control. He was a second lieutenant with a little less or a little more time in country than I had but not much. I made my way over to him, got his assessment of the situation, and then we made our best effort to get everybody out of there and get organized. We got a few NCOs together, whoever was left. We got whoever from Alpha Company would respond. And that was a mixed bag of everything from a wounded lieutenant to probably a couple of sergeants to probably a couple of Spec 4's. It was the ones that would respond, and we basically got together to get everybody loaded into tracks and get everybody out. We were going to pull out and put out a lot of suppressive fire with artillery batteries because we weren't that far from Santa Barbara, as I recall. I was talking to the tank company commander, and they were shooting. We had Hueys going in, we had my company shooting, I think my mortar platoon was probably set, so we're trying to get everybody together and we're trying to put a lot of suppressive fire on the rock pile." [29]

1ˢᵗ Lt James Brezovec states, "We were supposed to go up and basically get Alpha Company back off the mountain. We thought we were going to be part of an assault up Nui Ba Den, so that's what we heard. We never got up close enough to get into any of them. We went up and I think, mostly, we were trying to recover people from Alpha and bring them back." [30]

SP4 Jack Heick, C Company Mortar FO, says, "The mortar platoon leader, Lt. Dominic Stimola, asked me, 'Could you tell us where our low rounds are hitting?' They didn't want to hit Alpha Company at the base of the mountain. I told them that the rounds were hitting right where they are supposed to. They thanked me and said they would adjust from their position. I turned off the radio. The mortar platoon covered the entire mountainside through that day. They were careful of the jets, helicopters, and aircraft. They did an excellent job that day and almost emptied their load. I think we shouldn't forget their labor."[37]

Capt. Howard says, "The tanks were shooting over my head, and the company commander of Alpha Thirty-Fourth said, 'I'm sorry. I can't get off the road. These tanks are so big, I can't. I'll get bogged down, but I can stay here on the road and support you.' And so he was shooting over our head and all of a sudden he called me on the radio and he said, 'Have all your people get their heads down.' And I said, 'What are you talking about?' And he said, 'Just get your heads down now.' And about that time it sounded like the Third Avenue L was going overhead, and they had an eight-inch gun sitting on the road with them that was firing direct fire. You think a tank round going over your head is something; you ought to hear an eight-inch round! I mean, it was devastating. So once we got adjusted to that, we continued to use that as fire suppression along with the tanks, and I believe we had some Cobras and some artillery. My FO and I were coordinating most of that and trying to get everybody evacuated. We got everybody together, and we pulled back far enough so that we weren't taking any more direct fire."[29]

At 1705, the battalion log reads, "Total casualties 30 WIA, 3 KIA."[1]

A Charlie Company .50 gunner, Don Coughennower, realized that his barrel had worn out. He donned a pair of asbestos gloves and, in full view of the enemy on the mountain, removed the damaged barrel and replaced it with a new one.[38]

89

1st Lt. Mulhurn continues, "I noticed a couple of soldiers that appeared from out of the grass in front of me. They were Dennis Laken and Leonard Compton carrying the body of Captain Buckles, and they laid it almost at my feet. This was the most unnerving task that these soldiers would ever be called upon to do, and it showed in their faces. I was on the ground and called up to my track for a poncho to lay over him. The wind was blowing in gusts, and every time the poncho was blown off Buckles, a trooper would cease firing and lay it back over him."[8]

The line platoon tracks of Alpha began to move to the north. They stopped near the tanks. The medic track stayed close to the old medevac area until everyone from Alpha was gone. [7]

Doc D says, "Every one of the platoon medics [was] either killed or wounded that day. It was a day like one I never want to remember. The thing is, I guess—the main thing is, they sent us over to do a job that we could never have accomplished, but that didn't bother the guys, you know. They were there to do a job, and they were there to stand behind one another, and by God, they did it that day. As far as I'm concerned it's a group of heroes. God love 'em."[11]

Charlie Co had taken over the protection of the perimeter. Capt. Howard had called for all of the legs from Second Platoon to meet at the helipad and get on medevac detail.[29]

Forrest says, "As the Operations Officer, I was totally in the blind because I'm relying on communications from what's going on on the ground, and I'm not getting, even with Spec 4's running it, the kind of radio communication, and the radio traffic that I am getting doesn't paint the whole picture." [34]

The Battalion Log states, "5:30 - Blue Max departed Station."[1] Charlie Company was recovering Alpha wounded. The casualties appeared in a column on the right side of the battlefield, going away from it. It is estimated that they found thirteen wounded on the battlefield.[30]

Then the Battalion Log reads, "5:40 - A 2/2 closed FOB."[1] 2/6 found Mulhern on top of Capt. Buckles's command track. As the two began to talk, 2/6 told Mulhern that he thought the company had had it. He said, "I thought we were going to buy it right there." Mulhern was shot through the thigh and reported that he wanted to be dusted off; 2/6 was then the company commander. Knox found Mulhern.[8]

July 12 at 5:40 p.m.

Mike remembers, "At that time a round slapped me in the leg, and I spun around and fell, as did the soldier next to me. The soldiers around me were looking at me in that disbelieving look and shock on their faces. A shell-shocked soldier strode up to me and, seeing me on the ground with a medic cutting my pants off, he knelt down and he gave me a big bear hug and a kiss on the cheek. He looked me squarely in the eye and said, 'We're all gonna die, aren't we, sir?' I replied, 'That's bullshit. As far as I know, we're winning this thing. We have plenty of ammo and firepower, and help is on the way.'"[8]

Mike says, "I then heard the popping sound of a rapidly approaching chopper, and it descended right over me. A large, burly, cigar-chomping soldier jumped out of it and came over to me and said, 'What's up, sunny?' To which I replied, 'Basically we're getting the shit kicked out of us.' The soldier was Command Sgt. Maj. James Knox, and boy was I glad to see him. As the chopper ascended and passed over Buckles, the rotor wash blew the poncho off him again, and I could detect a real serious look on Top Knox's face."[8]

"Captain Buckles's body was still lying behind the commander's APC," remembers 2/6. "I decided that I had better get him dusted off. A young soldier who had only been in the company two days helped me carry him to the dustoff area. The helicopter door gunner yelled at me that they were only taking wounded—no bodies. I replied that this was our company commander. The gunner responded that he didn't care—wounded only. I continued to argue with him when he suddenly slumped over. He was dead with a bullet hole in his forehead."[7]

2/6 loaded the body of Capt. Buckles onto the helicopter.[7]

2/6 continues, "After I loaded the body, I ran to the front of the helicopter and told the copilot that his gunner was dead. He just shrugged his shoulders. I then gave him the thumbs-up to take off. Since he was overloaded, he put his nose down, slowly moved forward, bounced on the front of his skid a couple of times, and banked to his right. I could hear the popping of his rotor blade as he struggled to gain altitude."[7]

Shortly after this, as Streightiff was behind an APC, a bullet hit it and a piece of shrapnel lodged in his neck. He was immediately evacuated.[17] Gilliam was finally evacuated after spending most of the battle with a hole through his calf.[24]

Larry says, "I've been awful lucky. I feel I've been lucky, and I don't know why I made it, but I guess you always have your friends. And then you stop making friends because they didn't last long, you know. Years later you wonder—wonder about them and think about them, which is my problem for me to sit and think. It's not good, you know."[26]

"The way I feel is that when I left Vietnam, we was winning. That was my idea when I left. I thought we was doing fine and was winning the war, but I don't know what the hell happened after I left. You know, if we put twenty tracks on line shooting .50's and four of them with mortars in it, I mean, there's nothing going to stop us. If they wanted to win that damn thing, as far as I'm concerned, there never would have been a Ho Chi Min trail 'cause we would have just wiped it out."[26]

Heick says, "Captain Howard called for all the legs in Second Platoon to go on medevac detail. We all went there together, and when we got to the medevac area, we saw Major Kelly. (Note: We have looked for a Major Kelly for over eighteen years and cannot find him. There was a Captain Kelly there, but on July 13, Heick met with him and so this doesn't look like a confusable. B 1/2 was at the battle, and their battalion XO was Major Kelly, but he claims he was not at the base of the mountain. There was a brand new XO for the 2/2 named Maj. McDivitt, and he told us that he stayed in the TOC that evening. That leaves a major from the Twenty-Fifth. We have not found one that fits the qualification.) He told us, 'Grab stretchers and go find the wounded left on the battlefield.' They were shot in a column all the way to the base of the mountain. The medevac area was quite a ways from the base of the mountain, maybe three hundred meters. When we were carrying the wounded, we were as careful as we could be, but if we had a new man at the other end of the stretcher, we could hear a lot of bitching from the wounded we were carrying."[37]

Heick remembers, "When one chopper was full of wounded, it would take off. We put the dead under the shot-down chopper. They had a tarp over them. They were stacked [one] on top of another so it was hard to estimate how many we ended up with. We just assumed this was going to continue throughout the battle."[37]

Heick continues, "Medevacking is hard to do. We saw the brutal wounds that war inflicts, but it is also hard on the living. *Traumatic* is more like it. It made us scared that we might end up that way."[37]

Heick says, "My M-16 was double-feeding and jamming. I cleaned and oiled it, but it still jammed. I did this until I had heat exhaustion. A track had run over a tree, and I was resting on the track when Captain Howard said, 'It's getting late. See if you can get us out of here.' I said, 'Yes, sir!' and went back to find Major Kelly. He looked at me and said, 'Where's your flak jacket?' I told him Captain Howard wanted to know if we could pull out; it was getting late.[37]

"Maj. Kelley said I would have to ask the Alpha Company CO, and he showed me his location. I went there, and the men who wanted to talk to him were at port arms, so I did the same. When it came my turn, I said that it was getting late and Charlie Company wanted to pull out but it was up to him. He said that it was time and called over a guy that I suspect was the 1st Sgt. or next in command. He agreed and took down my name, rank, and service number on a matchbook cover. I saw the colonel standing with the major. He was there when the Alpha man gave me the explicit instructions."[37]

The Battalion Log says, "5:45, C 2/2 request Dust off" for 1 man WIA (Leo Schlotterer).[1] Leo was driving an APC when it was hit by small-arms fire, causing some shrapnel to hit Leo in the eyes. Leo was not to be dusted off until he went to the rear with the cooks from Charlie Company.[40]

Heick had made his way to the downed helicopter and replaced the M-60 gunner so the gunner could return to his crew. [37]

Capt. Howard recalls, "The first day, we got everybody gathered up, and it was dusk or a little later and we had the helicopter to secure. We had Alpha Company, and we were getting medical support for the wounded and counting heads and determined, I believe, that we were missing three people from Alpha Company. My best recollection is there were three bodies unaccounted for or three people unaccounted for, and they were presumed dead and in the battle site. And there were some tracks that had been abandoned there."[29]

Lugo remembers being in a track and seeing the red glow of the lamps. He thinks he was salvaging usable equipment.[35] Schlotterer remembers that after they removed the equipment, the track was destroyed where they were.[58] Heick says, "I pointed to the Command Post, and I saw them getting ready. I saw a large spool of wire rolling back. We started moving back a distance to blow the tracks, and I didn't see what happened next, but I seem to remember an explosion and a flash, but that was happening all day."[37]

Pilgrim recalled, "I'll never forget as I'm walking down the aisle of the hospital quonset hut at Cu Chi. I'm walking on a cream-colored foam mat, and there are beds on both sides. I remember how many of them said, 'Hi, Ron,' as I went by. I had no idea that there were that many guys from our company that had been hit that day. The doc took the bullet out of my arm but just cleaned the leg and left the bullet in there. He couldn't find it."[15]

Mike Mulhurn says, "I could then see that a chopper was landing around seventy-five meters in front of us. I thought, 'This must be where Joe's at,' and I surmised that the chopper had seen them from the air. To my surprise, the chopper rose from Joe's position, turned, and came in low to my position. The guys loaded me and the other wounded soldier onto the chopper, and we lifted off. We landed at the Twenty-Seventh Evac Hospital at Cu Chi, and the dead and wounded from Alpha were lined up in a row, laying the litters on the sidewalk. The medics pored over them and determined who needed the most urgent treatment."[8]

Phil says, "When we finally got off the mountain, we were given a section of the RON to guard for the night. We never got relieved. We usually—after a bad fight, we'd get relieved. We'd go back and regroup. Go back to base camp or go someplace and regroup. That night we went back about, like I said, maybe five hundred yards at the most, and we stayed right there and we ended up having what guys were left. And I'll betcha there were only two or three guys in each track. We had to make up squads for certain tracks. The drivers and the gunners we usually had, but we had to put some other guys with them. We spread them all out. Nobody was with anybody that day. We were at the front.[20]

"They brought in Charlie Company and stuck them over on the road. I had to walk over there to Captain Howard and talk to him. We talked about the next day. We went back to try to find them the next day. Of course, we went back. In fact, I led the group."[20]

Phil says, "Yes, I remember Sergeant Wullenweber. We talked later that night 'cause that's the reason why we talked is he thought he knew where the injured were and I knew where my three were. He thought he knew where those other guys—where the other guy was at. We talked about, I think, 'Well, why don't I just lead a squad of guys in?' Even during the day, I said, 'If we get some shit, we get some shit instead of announcing our presence with a hundred guys. Why don't I see if we can't just pick them up and get them out of there that way.' They said, 'No, we're going in all the way.' So, they did all right."[20]

Tennessee says, "I don't know how long I had been in the MASH unit when they was this damned butterball second lieutenant. He came in there saying, 'You look fine. You need to get back up there in the field. Your company is short of men and needs all the help they can get.' He told me I ain't hurt that bad and all that good shit. So they loaded Streightiff and some others back up, the ones they thought were able to fight again. They loaded us back up in trucks and took us back out to the RON where we were camped. I got out of the truck with a sling around one arm and a .45 in the other."[32] Bob says, "I remember so vividly that Tennessee was just—they never should have sent him back to the field. That night he just lay on the ground in excruciating pain." Tennessee passed out from the pain and was returned to the hospital, where he recovered for three weeks.[17]

July 12 at 5:59 p.m.

2/6 found the battalion commander and gave him a very brief report that did not include the Twenty-Fifth Infantry Division general being in the area that day. SP4 Bill Sly, from Awards and Decorations, had arrived and was given the task by Lt. Col. Vinson of interviewing the men of Alpha to see which ones should be put up for medals. Bill would spend the next few days interviewing the soldiers from Alpha who were left.[7]

Banks says, "I was told that my part of the perimeter would be in the rice field. I sat down in one foot of water and tried to get comfortable, even with the sniper fire coming in at all hours that night." Later that evening, he saw flashlights moving on the mountain. When the tanks saw the lights, they would slowly move their turrets and fire. The lights would be immediately extinguished.[19]

2/6 consolidated the company. No one above E-5 was left; Phil Deering is the exception, but when he met 2/6 that day, neither of them was wearing a shirt with rank on it. 1st Sgt Thomas was at Cu Chi hospital, and there were four unaccounted-for bodies. Lt. Col. Vinson stated that the battalion would go back the next day to find the bodies. One was found unharmed at Cu Chi Hospital two days later. The bodies of Cummins and King were found the next day, and one body (Kimmel) wasn't found until August 8, 1969.[7] Gilliam says, "But now this boy that got killed there, that Kimmel, he just come out there the day before. He stayed all night with us, and the next morning he got killed. He was just a young boy—well, we was all just boys. They would send them out there, and a lot of them didn't know where to turn around. They wasn't ready for it, I don't reckon. It's something I'll never forget."[24]

After everyone had left the mountain, it was covered with a flame bath. C-130 cargo planes flew slowly over the mountain and dumped fifty-five-gallon drums of fougasse (napalm).[41]

Charlie Company then formed a defensive perimeter with Alpha 2/2, Alpha 2/34, and the downed helicopter in the middle. They dug defensive positions and sent out LPs.[29]

The battalion TOC group began the arduous task of identifying all of the missing. They also began planning for the operations for the next day. Lt. Col. Vinson did not get any sleep that night. In a meeting between Vinson, Maj. Forrest, and Capt. Howard, it was agreed that Charlie Company would go back the next day and recover the three bodies, taking several of the Alpha troops to use as guides. Capt. Howard does not remember going to the battalion commander's track that night, and Forrest does not remember leaving the TOC, so this meeting probably took place early the next morning. [29]

Forrest says, "I did not go out that night but went out early the next morning. The reason for not going out that night is, for me to go out, I'd have to go out in my track or to take a number of vehicles to go out there to be reinforcing them. At that point, it was not necessary to reinforce them. Now I talked to Howard the next morning. I don't remember talking to him that night. I know I didn't talk to him that night, in person."[34]

July 12 at 6:57 p.m.

2/6 took possession of Capt. Buckles's command track. He radioed Top Jimmy Thomas back at Dau Tieng. The two men then started to match the company roster, trying to account for the exact disposition of each soldier, be they on R&R, wounded at the hospital in Cu Chi, KIA, located at Dau Tieng, or at FSB Buell. After two checks, four men were still unaccounted for. It was concluded that they were still back on the mountain and presumed dead.[7]

The task was completed about four o'clock on the morning of July 13, 1969. As 2/6 put down his roster, he remembered feeling more exhausted than at any other time in his life. "Alpha Company is gone. How can it ever be bought back to life before we're given yet another mission?"[7]

At ten thirty that night, Maj. Gen. Talbott, commander of the First Infantry Division, was informed that the 2/2 (Mech) had taken severe losses while attached to the Twenty-Fifth Infantry Division. He left his living quarters and called a meeting of his top aides at the First Infantry Division Operations Center. He was very concerned, and he called the Twenty-Fifth Infantry division commander, Maj. Gen. Hollis Williamson, to find out why they were sending First Infantry Division men into a battle instead of their own. He then called the II Field Force Corp Commander at Second Field Force, Maj. Gen. Ewell, to try to get his battalion back from the Twenty-Fifth. Ewell said that he would return the 2/2 (Mech) to the First Infantry Division as soon as possible.[43]

A battalion log entry states, "2245 Spooky 73 on station to work area of movement XT 2659."[1] Spooky was a gunship with mini guns on it. The coordinates indicate someone was trying to leave the mountain.

Late that night, 1st Sgt. Jimmy Thomas arrived at the RON site. He had been at the hospital counting casualties. He was very broken up because he thought he should have been in the field that day.[7]

Another battalion log entry reads, "2359 - Summary B 1/2 & A 2/34 supporting conducted BDA on B-52 strike. Neg Significant Report. A 2/2 conducted blocking force for B 1/2 then dismounted for BDA of additional area of B-52 strike. Encountered RPG & small arms resistance on Nui Ba Den. Sustained 9 KIA 37 WIA. *(My research has found 51 individuals that were reported WIA.)* Reinforced by A 2/34 & C 2/2 for withdrawal. A 2/2 company commander KIA. Journal Closed." George Forrest S-3[1]

So ends day one of intense fighting that will stay with us of the 2/2 (Mech) forever.[58]

Chapter 16: Alpha 2/2 (Mech) New Mission

Jack remembers, "The next morning, I awoke to the sound of Top shouting, '2/2, we are going back in!' I got my shirt, went over to the 2/1 track sore from head to toe. My lieutenant told me that I was again the forward observer, and I apologized for losing my radio. I got some magazines from Ron Getz—he had a full claymore bag full. I couldn't find mine, and I probably emptied them the day before. I readied myself and called the mortar platoon. They said our guns were down."[37]

Early on the morning of July 13, 1969, 2/6, Maj. George Forrest (on his second tour; his first included the Ia Drang Battle), and Gen. Henderson were in a conversation. When informed that Lt. Col. Vinson had elected to send Charlie Company out to retrieve the four Alpha Company bodies, BG Henderson argued that Alpha should go themselves. When 2/6 informed the general that Alpha didn't have the manpower to do the task, BG Henderson called 2/6 a coward. Maj. Forrest got between the two men and informed BG Henderson that he agreed with 2/6 and that he knew for a fact that 2/6 was not a coward.[7]

July 13 at 7:00 a.m.

Maj. Gen. Talbott arrived at the TOC. He walked up to Lt. Col. Vinson and asked him why he had ordered his men to go up a mountain. When he was told that Vinson had received a direct order to do so, he then asked, "By whom?" When he was told that the order had come from Col. Hayward of the Twenty-Fifth Infantry Division, Maj. Gen. Talbott walked over to the colonel, and the two of them had a very intense, private talk.[41] Years later, Capt. Combs confided that he always excused himself and never listened to Talbot's conversations with other officers, but judging from the tone, he had never heard a general talk to an officer like that.[43]

After the intense talk, Col. Hayward walked over to Lt. Col. Vinson and said, "Well, that was bad. You know, you win some and you lose some," and then he walked away.[41]

In a letter to his wife, Newell Vinson noted that Maj. Gen. Hollis Williamson and BG Davis Henderson of the Twenty-Fifth Division did not seem too upset about the loss of life. Newell did not learn of the part that BG Henderson had played in the battle until the summer of 1995.[41]

After meeting with the generals, Lt. Col. Vinson and Maj. Forrest visited the RON site to review the day's events with the officers. They informed Capt. Howard that there were four bodies near the mountain that had to be found, and they told Alpha to go to Fire Support Base Santa Barbara to pick up an eight-inch gun.[41]

Drivers and gunners were about all that remained of Alpha Company. They proceeded to FSB Santa Barbara to pick up a self-propelled eight-inch howitzer along with four or five trucks loaded with two-hundred-pound shells. 2/6 pulled point. As he looked back, he saw a long line of APCs, most with only a driver and a gunner. About halfway to the base, some senior Twenty-Fifth Division officer came up on the company net. "You need to stop and clear the road of mines," he barked. The road was filled with heavy Vietnamese traffic—lumber trucks, motor scooters, Lambrettas filled with pimps and their prostitutes, and ox-drawn carts creating a huge traffic jam. In the First Division area of operations, such traffic was an indication that no enemy was present. Probably half of the people on the road were Viet Cong who mingled with the others Vietnamese. All the American column had to do was stay in the tracks of the Vietnamese vehicles.[7]

July 13 at 8:02 a.m.

2/6 ignored the Twenty-Fifth Division officer and directed Lt. Mathews to call the artillery battery at Santa Barbara for a possible fire mission. As soon as the artillery battery broadcast its readiness to fire, all helicopters and aircraft knew to clear the area. The command helicopter from which the order to clear the mines had come fled the area with its radio transmission still squawking![7]

Alpha Company arrived at Nui Ba Den at about ten o'clock with the eight-inch gun and five ammunition trucks. The eight-inch gun, some 155s, and all nine of the tanks began firing a prep for Charlie to go in and extract the bodies. At least five members of Alpha were taken aboard various tracks to act as guides. They were Wully, Deering, Chief, James Hale, and Dan King.[20] Lt. Col. Vinson and Command Sgt. Maj. Knox decided to go with Charlie. Capt. Howard made both of them take off their helmets and replaced them with generic helmets without rank. Knox began organizing people to do all the tasks assigned that day.[29]

Chapter 17: Charlie Company Mission

July 13 at 10:00 a.m.

Capt. Howard says, "We blew two tracks on the second day—one of ours had been hit in the road wheels and one of Alpha's that had landed upside down in a bomb crater. We went in and stripped them of all their radios and all the other stuff the second day."[29]

Capt. Howard continues, "Command Sgt. Maj. Knox linked up with us on July 12; actually, he almost ground guided my company. He went in with me again the next day. In fact, on the second day, I made him take off his sergeant major helmet and put on a blank one. He rode on the back of my track. We had the ramps down because we were going in and we were going to try to make it fast and recover whatever we could and get out. And he rode on the back of one of my tracks. He was absolutely—I don't know if he was fearless or if he was just being a good leader, but he got highly irritated that I made him take off his sergeant major's helmet and put on a nondescript one. But he did it nonetheless. His biggest effort both of those days was organizing people and getting them to do what needed to be done, which was to load wounded or dead onto the helicopters or the back of tracks, to pick up their radios and their rifles and their equipment, and to get organized and to get moving. He did what a senior NCO should do."[29]

About eleven o'clock that morning, Charlie Company was on line and going toward the mountain when the tanks and the eight-inch opened up, firing salvos. All who were there remembered the sound and feel of the large shells going over their heads at greater than the speed of sound. Vinson recounted, "When we kicked off our departure line, they fired over the top of us and I think every track stopped in its tracks because we had never had fire over the top of us at that close range. It was absolutely amazing."[29]

When the company finally reached the tree line, Charlie Company opened up with everything that they had. Vinson remembered, "I was kind of riding as a rider with Captain Howard. Captain Howard was handling his company, doing well, and there was no reason for me to interfere with that. I felt like kind of a spare tire."[41]

July 13 at 11:00 a.m. The battle site had become a very visible place, and there were a number of one- and two-star generals overhead watching the progress. The orders for the day were to rescue the four bodies that were left on the field of battle and to destroy the APC that was in the B-52 bomb crater and the APC that couldn't move out of the mud.[29]

Phil says, "I did not get dusted off until the thirteenth. I went back to the base camp and so forth. I never got shot, exactly, through the leg. The bullet went down my calf and exited my right leg straight on down. The wound was probably about four or five inches long."[20]

Phil continues, "Wullenweber and I were the two sergeants then on the thirteenth. Because the three killed that were around me at the time, I knew exactly where they were and I said, 'Well, I'll take you on in.' I had this stupid white bandage around my leg that Doc had put on, and I'm walking here with this bandage and two other radio guys. They would be walking beside the tracks and the outgoing fire was going on and nothing's coming in, and all of a sudden *zip, zip, zip*. I says, 'Well, you know what, you can tell those guys you've got incoming coming in now, Jesus Christ.' I started getting behind the damn tracks then. The bullets were hitting the ground right next to me ... and I thought, 'What, a stupid thing. You're walking with two radio guys and a white bandage around your leg and you're trying to find these bodies like nobody's up there going to shoot at you.' In all honesty, we didn't really think anybody was really going to be there the first day, and the next day we lost two more guys. I couldn't believe it."[20]

Lt. Jim Brezovec remembers the morning of the thirteenth of July. "Well, my platoon wound up in an oddball little detail. We had to blow up the remains of an armored vehicle that was in a B-52 bomb hole. Yeah, I remember, and we went in—me and a Sergeant Green and an Alpha Company sergeant went in there—and we rigged it up with C4 and multiple fuses because we had no intention of going back into the area, and the whole idea was to make sure the NVA didn't recover anything they could use from it. And then we had a little bit of a predicament because about the time we got the fuses pulled, somebody started peppering at us. Somebody started sniping at us."[30]

Jim continues, "Once we dropped down into the hole, it was pretty hard for anybody actually to get a good shot at us. The hole was real deep. But anyway, we fused that thing up, and we drew a lot of fire when we went down in there. So now we had a new predicament. The fuses were going. And we were being shot at. Finally we decided, 'Well, if we stay here, we're going to get blown up for sure.' The other alternative was to get over the back lip of this hole and run like hell for the high grass, which is what we did. We made it without any problems or else they'd stopped firing."[30]

Capt. Howard remembers, "They blew them up with that pointed bucket. That was our standard. I think over a period of time I probably blew up six or maybe eight M113 A1s over there because in the heat of battle, the hull got cracked or for whatever reason it was, it was a legitimate reason under the rules of the time. But C4 and shape charges, large quantities of which I carried in my company—I had a couple of guys who were wizards with explosives. There was a lot of individual heroism both of those days and a lot of different, little private things that went on. It was not your conventional kind of operation. It was not like, There's the enemy and we're going to attack them and then circle them or whatever. We were trying to do several missions. We were going to retrieve some bodies, we were trying to make sure some valuable property, equipment didn't fall into enemy hands, and we were trying to do each of those things without anybody getting hurt. Now obviously that didn't work out very well."[29]

Other members of Charlie were trying to find equipment that was left on the field. Lombardi was given the mission of finding Kimmel, and although he made a diligent search, he did not find him.[36] Jim Hale of A 2/2 did find Kimmel's body; he was lying face down, but he had on a very distinct gold watch that his father had given him, and Hale was trying to get the attention of two of Charlie's soldiers who were carrying a stretcher. Before he could lead them to the body, Jim was run over by a Charlie Company APC that was backing up and was wounded. He was taken to the helipad for a dustoff to Cu Chi. At the MASH unit, Hale was X-rayed and told that he would be very sore for a while, but there were no broken bones. They did dope him up and had him go across the street to a tent to rest.[26] Lombardi's men noticed that they were receiving fire from the trees off to their left. Lombardi had the whole squad open up on the trees, and they saw an NVA fall to the ground.[36]

In the intense fire, SP4 John Belvin, SP4 Otis Gadd, and PFC Haywood Shearing of Charlie 2/2 were all wounded. Belvin was the driver of a track that was hit by an RPG. His gunner was seriously wounded, so Belvin manned the .50 until he was relieved and carried off the track.[57] Sgt. Lombardi and his squad blew the damaged track in place.[36] SP4 Franklin Whaley's .50-caliber machine gun was damaged by an enemy round. He picked up an M-79 and continued firing at the enemy on the mountain.[59] SP4 Larry Reeves, a medic, saw the wounded men on the ground and applied first aid to them until they could be evacuated.[60]

July 13 at 11:50 a.m.

Lugo's men found the first casualty from the day before. PFC Ralph Hoover reached the casualty and, in full view of the enemy, hauled the body back to his track.[61] SP4 Louis Stoudt was a driver that day. He helped his machine gunner spot enemy positions throughout the duration of the battle.[62]

Jim wonders, "When we moved up the next morning after our little escapade with the track, we came back and rejoined the unit and continued moving up. That's when I lost two guys that morning. We lost two of them. Both of those guys had less than a week to go in the field. They were going back to the rear and then they would have gone home in about three weeks. One was named Squirrel, and I remember the other one was Bradbury."[30]

Steven Bradbury, a twenty-year-old .50 gunner from Wichita, Kansas, was shot and killed.[54] Others remembered him as long and lean and kind of quiet, a man with a good sense of humor.[30]

Doc Baehr recalls, "SP4 Robert Worrell, a twenty-year-old .50 gunner from Portsmouth, Virginia, was shot and killed.[55] He was well liked by the members of his platoon. He was short and very outgoing."[30]

Doc Baehr says, "The .50 gunner on my track, Worrell—his nickname was Squirrel—was killed right in front of me. The other one that was killed was Steve Bradbury. Bradbury and Wurrell were shot right through the heart. I would say it was relatively small group of people shooting at us because the shots were more aimed; it wasn't a big sporadic blast coming from all directions."[39]

The second body from the day before was sighted and brought aboard one of the tracks. SP4 Don Coughennower, a Third Platoon .50 gunner, realized that the .50 gunners were being targeted by the snipers on the mountain.[38]

July 13 at 1:00 p.m.

Command Sgt. Maj. Knox mounted the .50 and began to fire at the mountain. When that wore out, he picked up an M-79 and continued firing.[63] Doc Baehr, Charlie Company's medic, went to the track and inspected Squirrel's wound. Squirrel had been hit through the chest.[39]

Charlie Company completed the mission except for finding Kimmel and began an orderly withdrawal.[29] Coughennower was one of the few .50 gunners who made sure that his gun could fire to the rear. As the company departed, his track was the last to leave the mountain.[38] His driver, SP4 Tom Stillwell, held the APC steady as the enemy fire became concentrated on the one remaining track.[64]

The men of Charlie Company called this day "the day the Virgin got her due" or "the day the Black Bitch got her due."[35]

Charlie Company got back to the RON site. Doc Baehr tagged both Bradbury and Worrell. Doc Baehr says, "I had both of them on stretchers, and I had ponchos all around Worrell and Bradbury. I remember Bradbury always wore his dog tag in his shoes, right in his shoelaces."[39] Coughennower noticed that he had sweated through his fatigue pants. "At least I think it was sweat," he reports.[38]

July 13 at 2:00 p.m. According to Heick, a Twenty-Fifth Infantry general was angry that they had not picked up the last body, and the general was saying that C 2/2 should fight to the last man rather than leave any dead on the field. Larry, the 2-1 gunner, stood up and with his M-16 in his hand, stated, "I'll kill you first." The general asked who there was a friend of Larry's, and when Heick said he was, the general ordered Heick to make sure that no one shot him that day. Heick and Larry went to Capt. Tom Kelly, who calmed Larry down.[37]

Jim says, "We had four bodies laid out on the berm, two of ours and two from Alpha Company."[30]

According to Lombardi, one of the gunners from Charlie was very upset over losing two of his friends. When he checked his gun, he noticed that only a few rounds were left on the belt of his .50. He threw them down in anger, and just then a Twenty-Fifth colonel walked by and saw him. The colonel ordered the gunner to pick up the discarded ammo. The gunner refused, and when the colonel got adamant, the gunner replaced the ammo with a new belt and locked and loaded on the colonel. The colonel went to get Capt. Howard, and by the time they got back, the entire squad was there in support of the gunner. Capt. Howard explained to the colonel that his men were angry over losing two of their friends and that it would be better just to let it drop. The two walked away.[36]

Brezovec saw that four American bodies were laid out in a line, and a colonel was running around the area. The colonel was bitching about policing up the area because some general had wanted to view the bodies. One of the .50 gunners was angry that his buddies were being put on display, and he locked and loaded on the colonel. Jim ran up to the man and said. "Look, don't do this. It isn't worth a trip to Leavenworth." He finally talked the man off the APC and calmed him down.[30]

Jim recalls, "What I remember happening that day was being in the hole and blowing up the tracks. Making the advance to get to wherever we got, we were mostly in high grass and one sergeant of mine from National Guard Unit—we picked him up as an extra. He's from Canada, was wounded, and I was running around trying to help him like an idiot, getting in the line of fire. He was walking when he got hit in the shoulder, and he wasn't able to get back to an aid station anyway. That was the problem. Then we went back and they had four bodies laid out, and I remember losing my temper about the whole thing because some idiot colonel was running around there." Jim adds, "He was a fool. Full bird—he was running around bitching about policing up around the bodies because the general was coming or something. He has my vote for idiot of the week award."[30]

110

Soon everyone's attention was again on the mountain as it was peppered with napalm, fougasse, and CS gas. (CS is really very tiny crystals that make breathing very uncomfortable.)[29]

Around three in the afternoon, the recon platoon and the battalion command tracks arrived at the RON site. They had with them Gilliam and other Alpha soldiers who hadn't been badly wounded.[1]

Chapter 18: Back to Buell

With their arrival, Alpha Company was sent back to FSB Buell to reequip and to get more personnel.[7]

Some people's anger could be considered ice cold; others may be red hot. Mike Mirenda's anger over this situation was volcanic.[12] His anger erupted from him. He told me, "That's because that son-of-a-bitching general. I was going to shoot the bastard afterward, when he landed later that night. Man, it took six guys to hold me down because I was going to kill him. He knew the NVA were dug in there; otherwise, they wouldn't have put a B-52 strike in there. That's why I was screaming at the frickin' general.

"He knew that the NVA owned the middle of that mountain. We had the top and the bottom, but it was just suicide to try to go up. That stupid bastard. I understand he got sent to the Pentagon after this mistake, pushing pencils. Well, I hope he was pushing toilet paper because he was full of shit.

"When I went to Vietnam and I had about ten months left in the army, I was sent to the Headquarters Company to repair radios. I had learned to do that in the army. This captain that we had before Buckles, he had a radio break down when his regular guy was on R&R, so they sent me to repair it. I fixed him up real nice and good. He was happy with my work, so he shanghaied me to Alpha Company. I was not exactly pleased about the whole thing, and I let him know it. We never saw eye to eye on a lot of things."

Mirenda says, "Now Buckles was different. He was a good guy, a pretty decent officer. He was Armor; he wasn't Infantry. I think that he was on the major's list. There were a lot of officers that were just ticket punchers, but not him. He was not, believe me; he was not a ticket puncher. He trusted me with a lot of stuff and let me do things my way, as long as they got done.

"Normally I wouldn't have been with him. But he said, 'Come on, throw the radio on. You're coming with me today.' You see, his regular radio guy was on R&R, and he wanted me because he knew what I could do. I don't think that he was figuring on getting killed at all. He did tell me to be real careful because he didn't have a real good feeling about going up that mountain."

Mirenda adds, "That mountain was some kind of mountain. It was—what?—a mile in one direction and about a quarter of a mile to half a mile in the other. They had some mammoth caves in there. I'd be surprised if they didn't have whole ammo dumps in there. I mean, they had water; they had tunnels that went out under the roads. I even heard that they even had a hospital in the middle of that damn mountain.

"I was with the lead element that went up that mountain. We got to a point about 110 meters up, and that's when all the shit broke loose. Capt. Buckles knew we couldn't go forward or to either side, so he ordered us to retreat. We were told to retreat, so we started backing off. We had some cover fire from the tanks, and I think that they did put some artillery rounds up there, but that was higher up. Most of the fire was from the tanks and then the .50s when the tracks moved up.

"We hit the bottom of the mountain. In fact, he and I hit one bomb crater at the same time—you know, in one side and then right out then other. When we got to the elephant grass he stood up like John Wayne. Usually he was pretty cautious, but not that fight. Right after he got hit, I took a round, the radio took a round. That's when I said, 'Oh, shit,' and then I decided I had better do something quickly.

"I started back to find a radio. I came upon this black sergeant, Sgt. First Class Stewart. He had been hit in the right arm. He was in pain, and there was a real hole taken out of his elbow. So I took his boot lace off and put a tourniquet on him so we could get him back to the medevac area. I pulled him back a little, and then we could see some medics, someone to help him further. We got a couple of other guys, and we kind of like threw him into the helicopter."

Mirenda continues, "One of the people that I remember from that day was S. Sgt. Phil Deering. He was an instant NCO and about our age, but he was everywhere that day. He was good. Phil was one of the best combat guys you ever want to have. He had been hit early in the battle, but he didn't let that bother him. He just kept going.

"I still had to get to the tracks to get to the radio. I needed to get communications going with the battalion so they knew what was going on. I got to the Old Man's track, and I got on top of it and began coordinating everything. Nobody else could; they had all been hit. I just got on the horn and tried to get anybody I could think of. I mean, we had lots of wounded people.

"I saw this helicopter land, and as he came down, about seven bullets went through the back of his helicopter. I got on the radio and said, 'You've just been hit seven times in the tail.' The copter pilot came on and asked, 'Is the tail rotor still turning?' I said, 'Yeah.' He said, 'Then everything is still okay.' He came back two or three more times. I just don't know how they did that.

"Finally Lt. Mulhern got to the track. I was on top directing things when he got hit in the leg. We got his ass onto the copter and told him not to worry because he wanted to stay.

"I was ready to kill that general. After we pulled into the fire support base, a television crew comes in and someone sent them out to me because we only had one second lieutenant left. They sent the crew out to me and they said. 'How do you feel about these people getting killed?'"

I said, "Get the fuck out of here before I kill you. I'm going to put a grenade in your fucking shorts and pull the pin. 'The television crew went back to Major Mead and reported what had happened and when he heard what they had asked me, he said, 'You what? All right, from now on, just stay away from that man over there.' We never saw ABC again."[12]

2/2(Mech) was visited by a television camera crew. The crew stated that the footage they shot might be shown on ABC.

Sgt. Lombardi said, "My father says he knows I'm on TV because he yelled at me. He said, 'I seen you on TV. What the hell were you doing without your helmet on? You have a pair of sunglasses,' he said. 'Damn you, you're standing up there with a goddamn 60, and you don't have a helmet on. They're firing,' he said. 'What were you doing?' I said, 'Oh, Christ, I forgot that.' And I did. I actually was up there standing with a 60 because the .50 had burned out. I was up there without a helmet, trying to cover while we were changing the barrel of the 50; my hair's blowing. We all had to have a sense of humor. I never worried about it.[36]

Doc Baehr says, "It's the only one fight that I was in that we got beat."[39]

Bill tells Maj. Forrest, "So the story that I think I'm going to end up with is the story of the courage of the leaderless people on the ground."[34]

Forrest replies, "That's a good tack because, I think—and I know you've read Joe's book, Joe and Hal Moore's book— if you focus on the courage of these kids and what they did, that comes across better than if you highlight the big screwup that it really was. I'm not saying downplay the screwup because it was, in fact, a screwup. But if you home in on what happens after Buckles is lost, that's what your book owes those nine guys or those eleven guys or those forty-one guys—some dignity, some courage, some soldierly kind of memory."[34]

Forrest says, "My paragraph would sound like: 'These were the best of America's young people who went and did what their country expected them to do with dignity, with honor, with bravery, all those kinds of things, at great sacrifice, and they need to be remembered for that. They need to be remembered because when, as Gen. Moore says, "When it came time for them to perform, not for democracy or some grand political scheme, it was for my buddy." Those guys went back on the hill not because they believed in some domino theory. Those guys went back because Buckles was up there, their NCOs were up there, and a bunch of other guys that they had grown up with, matured with, suffered with, laughed with, cried with, got drunk with. That's what this war was really all about."[34]

Forrest can't remember ever having gone into a battle or a firefight saying, "Geez, I'm doing this to protect the American way of life." He says, "I guess, as I get older and I get more involved with guys who were there, I'm beginning to realize that the sacrifices that these guys made—again not for some grand scheme—was because, 'I know that this is my buddy over here.' As you read Gen. Moore's book, one of the characters in that book that stands out more than anything else is Bill Beck. Bill Beck talks about, 'I put my life on the line for my buddy who got shot in the head. That's who I put my life on the line for.' Not for Westmoreland or whoever the hell else was in charge."[34]

In an e-mail sent to 2/6 years after the battle from Lt. Gen. Larry Jordan is the following statement: "The Battle at Nui Ba Den, The Black Virgin Mountain, was an unnecessary, bloody, and poorly planned battle that witnessed the utmost in bravery, valor, and duty by American Soldiers."[7]

So ended the day of July 13, 1969, and so ended two days of intense fighting.[58]

Chapter 19: After the Battle

Early in the morning of July 14, a battalion chaplain, Capt. Gary Baxter, held a memorial service for the dead of Alpha Company.[65]

By noon, replacements arrived for Alpha. They included Capt. Smith, Lt. Raddtz, Lt. Papov, Lt. Williams, and fifty enlisted men.[41]

By one thirty, a change-of-command ceremony was held for the new company commander, Capt. Smith. The battalion was visited by Maj. Gen. Talbott, commanding general of the First Infantry Division; Brig. Gen. Wolff, ADC First Infantry Division; and Col. Post, First Brigade commander.[41]

Later that evening, Vinson was informed that he had won a new Ford Mustang that had been raffled off by the First Infantry Division Scholarship Fund. The mountain took another beating from the B-52 again that night.[41]

July 14 at 12:00 p.m., after the battle

Phil says, "It's a hell of a big mountain. That was a mountain made by God, that's for sure. Ours was definitely not a very coordinated effort. I mean, militarily, strategy was poor. It really was. It was very poor. I think they thought they had enough firepower in case something would happen, but the firepower wasn't set up right for it to happen. And also the mountain wasn't meant to be taken by whole companies of men. To me, that was a mountain that you wanted to send LRRPs (long-range reconnaissance patrols) up and see what's going on. The men on the hill that day, they stuck together well—very well. I give a lot of credit to the drivers and the .50 gunners that started pulling up, and I think a lot of—I know that the ones that I directed, they were doing it individually. I mean, they were coming and they were just waiting for somebody to tell them where to go and what to do. They performed outstandingly because I tell you what, they became the prime focus of most of the fire, the sniper fire and stuff. They became the primary target, and they just hung in there. The guys that I worked with—and they hung in there the whole time—and they just, they hung right in there. And even if you were a .50 gunner, you're still hanging out there."[20]

In the morning of July 16, Alpha went out for the first time with the new soldiers. Vinson informed Col. Post that the Awards and Decorations people had spent three days writing citations for the men of Alpha Company. He requested that one of the division's generals come out the next day and have an impact awards ceremony.[41] This meant that the awards were automatically approved and the paperwork would be expedited.[58]

When Vinson had taken over command of the battalion, he had made some changes in the SOP during a battle. In his words, "When a company got into contact, the word then was, 'Pile on.' The first thing they called for was ammo and for resupply. When those helicopters went in, the people that were to go with them were the historical people, the awards people, and the chaplain—that's Father Aloysuis Nundorf, a super soldier, chaplain, everything you'd ever want.[41]

"I got a lot of flak from that, from the S-1, but I explained to them that this is a historical record. I wanted the decorations to be from firsthand accounts, and I wanted the decorations ceremony to take place right after the action."[41]

Vinson recounted that the battalion was supported by thirty-seven howitzers, nine tank cannons, over twenty-five air strikes, and forty heavy machine guns. After that fight, there was no enemy activity in the Twenty-Fifth Division Area for at least a week.[4]

The Twenty-Fifth Division contacted Vinson and asked what enemy body count he wanted. They told him he could pick any number up to a couple hundred. Vinson picked forty-two.[41]

Hale says, "After resting for a couple of days, I was told to find my way back to my company. I found a convoy headed for Lai Khe. One of the truckers needed a soldier to ride shotgun, so I got aboard. We arrived in Lai Khe in time for me to catch a helicopter ride out with the cooks. And I was assigned to ride in Wully's track."[26]

Vinson sent a copy of the battle as written by the *Stars and Stripes* to his wife, but he warned her not to believe it. He said, "The media must be covering a different war. We were continually engaged and the coverage was obviously of us, but it was so inaccurate that I could barely recognize the activity. When reporters rely on press briefings given in Saigon, they are reporting on news that has been reviewed and altered a number of times." Many of the men saw the write-ups in various newspapers. Most were very upset that the newspapers made it sound like a great victory.[41]

**July 17 at
2:00 p.m.**

Sgt. Lombardi recalls, "The biggest joke was that my mother sent me a newspaper clipping later. She knew that we were in combat and it claimed a big victory. Some guy said it looked like hitting a rock against a log and the ants are popping out. I figured, 'What battle was this? Where the hell is this?' All I remember is they said it was a victory and I said, 'Who the hell wrote this?' You know, I don't want to write home to Mom saying we got our asses kicked. I didn't want to say, 'Mom, we got our butts kicked, and I'm lucky to go home alive.'"[36]

Vinson wrote to the *Stars and Stripes* and told them that the only thing that they got right was the unit, the date, and the location. Everything else in their article was wrong.[41]

Tennessee says, "It wasn't until later that they sent me to the big hospital in Cu Chi. I stayed there for two or three weeks before I got back to my company. When I got there, they tried to give me the M-79, and I said, 'I had it, didn't like it, don't want it.' So I wound up with an M-16."[32]

On the morning of July 17, 2/6 went to Cu Chi Hospital to see the wounded. The only one there was Mulhern. The two of them traveled back to Dau Tieng, where Mulhern became the XO of Delta Company. 2/6 became the recon platoon leader, a position normally filled by the best and most senior first lieutenant, not a second lieutenant.[7]

On the afternoon of July 18, Maj. Gen. Talbott, with his aide, Capt. Combs (former Alpha Company Commander), awarded two Silver Stars, three Bronze Stars for Valor, and three ACMs with V (for valor) for the men of Alpha 2/2 (Mech). The battalion's combat photographer, SP4 Daniel Moilanen, recorded the event with his camera.[58] Van remembered that at the ceremony, he heard someone say, "If this keeps up, Alpha 2/2 will be the most decorated company in Vietnam."[14]

Pete recalls, "First of all, I am not seeking any publication for myself ever for any reason. But if anybody ever wants to quote me, they damn well can. It has to do with what I said about Hamburger Hill. There were times in that war when we, 'we' being the chain of command, lost perspective, and in an attempt to run down a group of enemy soldiers and cause them to be casualties, we forgot what price we might have to pay. Those of us who cut enough brush knew that you can get in a situation very quickly where one enemy casualty meant one US casualty, and that was just not the way it ought to be. What we needed to do, particularly at that stage of the war, was make the enemy come to us, deny him freedom of movement, deny him food, and deny him the capability to fight on. We pretty well did that, but periodically, and it happened to me when I was a company commander (I had my own ways of dealing with it), I would get somebody in a helicopter who was senior to me telling me that I should dismount a squad, go across a stream, and dig this little guy out of a hole there. A couple of times I even got yelled at for not doing that. I never got yelled at by Michienzi, and that's the guy who counted to me at the time."[43]

On July 20, 1969, the 4.2 mortar platoon spotted two NVA digging on Nui Cau. They laid fifteen rounds on target, setting off two secondary explosions. Col. Vinson noted in a letter to his wife that he was getting tired of the rainy season. They were getting heavy rain most every day, usually in the late afternoon. The radio reported that man had finally landed on the moon. Listeners heard those now famous words, "One small step for man, one giant leap for mankind."[41]

On July 21, 1969, the 2/2 (Mech) was finally returned to the control of the First Infantry Division.[4]

On the twenty-sixth of that month, Lt. Col. Vinson conducted an investigation to see if they could determine the whereabouts of Kimmel's body. Van, Hippie, Al, Sammy Labastida, Jim Hale, and others were called in to tell their stories. They were able to trace Kimmel all the way through, and they realized that he was in the tall grass, not at the base of the mountain.[41]

On August 5, tracker dogs were sent to the mountain to try to find Kimmel. On August 8, a helicopter with Gilliam and other men from the 2/2 (Mech) returned to the battle site and found Kimmel's remains because they saw the sun reflect off his watch. There was no fire coming from the mountain that day.[24]

Doc Baehr says, "On my first day in the field, Bob Wurrell, he was the one that—we got in a firefight and he grabbed me. Because that day, when the medics come into the country, we were supposed to be given a week of orientation with a doctor. I was talking to the doctor, and he's our company commander as far as the medics go. And I got off the chopper, and I had talked to him. I just introduced myself: 'Okay, I'm here, and I'm a medic,' so okay. I could see that over on the other side of the hill there was smoke, and there was a battle going on not that far from the fire support base.

"And then they came in with two tracks, and then they started unloading the wounded. And when they unloaded the first one, he said, 'Geez, that's a medic.' And he unloaded the next one and said, 'Geez, that's another medic,' and he had his arm blown off. And then this first sergeant who I can't remember his name said, 'Well, we got to go back.' And the doctor said, 'You've got to go. I'm sorry, but you got to go.' And originally when I got there, he says, 'You're going to be going to Bravo Company. That's the company you're going to be going with 'cause they got some medics that are due back home.' And here he come in with two medics from Charlie Company and one had lost his arm, and I remember that his arm was laying on the stretcher between his legs.

August 17 at 12:00 p.m.

"When I got out to Charlie Company, I got off this track and Squirrel grabbed me and said, '"Get down behind this tree. Don't try to be a hero.' From there on, we were real close, and when I got to be the senior medic, which you get your own track, and then as soon as the gunner went home, I got him on there as a gunner and the driver was Ken Cook. Now he was from Colorado. But anyway, that's how I got introduced to it, and that's how we got to be friends with the Squirrel. He wasn't very big. He had kind of a little potbelly on him, which was unusual for a younger kid. But he had kind of a little beer belly or something. And he was blonde—real blonde hair." [39]

Capt. Howard says, "I can honestly tell you that, for whatever reason, when I got to Vietnam, it was almost like, 'Finally,' even though I was concerned about it. I had been 'preparing' for about eight or nine years when I got to Vietnam. While I had the usual concerns about, 'Is it morally right to kill people?' all that crap went away when the first round went over my head. 'Whoa, that son-of-a-bitch is trying to kill me.' But, and I hope this doesn't sound wrong, but I enjoyed my year in Vietnam because I felt like I was able to bring some people home that might have died otherwise. But I mean, God, what an exciting year. What a time." [29]

Jerry says, "Well, you know, of course, they bombed the hell out of the mountain the night before. I didn't expect too much. And, boy, we got our butt whipped on that one, you know. And then right on the *Stars and Stripes* it stated that we won that battle. I said, 'My God, if we won that one, there's something a matter with them.' That was the stupidest thing anybody could have ever done—try to climb a mountain with people in there. That was the stupidest. I mean, we had a general tell us to do that.' [33]

Nov 15 at 1:00 p.m.

Late in November of 1969, Bill was asked by the new battalion commander, Lt. Col. Brown, to make notes on the history of the battalion. A lieutenant was going to complete the notes. As the time to complete the history drew near, it became obvious that Bill's notes had better be in great shape. The afternoon before the history was due, the lieutenant asked for the notes. Bill had left the two days in July out of the history because he thought he was supposed to. No one had given him any direction on this.

When the history of the battalion was completed, Bill's notes appeared verbatim.[58]

On November 23, 1969, the Twenty-Fifth Infantry Division started the first of three operations to rid Nui Ba Den of the NVA. The three were called Cliffdweller I, II, and IV. [2]

The Twenty-Fifth Infantry Division After Action Reports written November 24, 1969, include the following:

> 121305 Jul 69 - At xt273604, Co A 2-2 Inf (M) received heavy small arms and RPG fire from an estimated company. Returned fire with organic weapons, LFT, artillery, air strikes, and Flame Bath. Fire ceased at 1730. US losses: 8 KIA, 32 WIA. Enemy losses: 11 KIA (BC).

> 131202 Jul 69 - Co A, 2/2 Inf (M) received sniper fire at XT 277607 and returned fire with organic weapons, LFT, artillery, and air strikes. US losses: 2 KIA, 2 WIA. Enemy losses 10 KIA (BC).

In the "Lessons to Be Learned" section of the Twenty-Fifth Infantry Division After Action Reports, the dates go from July 11 to July 14, completely missing the two days of this battle.2

In the "Lessons Learned" section of Lt. Col. Vinson's report about the four months that he had been battalion commander from June 9, 1969, to October 10, 1969, he stated that his battalion had killed 860 enemies at a cost of 18 US KIAs. Other than this battle, the men of the 2/2 (Mech) had killed 818 enemies at a cost of 7 US KIAs. While any loss is terrible, a kill ratio of 117 to 1 is remarkable.[4]

The First Infantry Division Yearbook for the year 1969 makes no mention of any battle on July 12 and 13, 1969. The 2/2 (Mech) section appears verbatim as it did in the "History of the Battalion."[5]

The Twenty-Fifth Infantry Division Yearbook with a date of September 1968 to September 1969 stated the following: "Throughout July and August, the enemy remained quiet around the foot of Nui Ba Den. Contact was sporadic as squads and enemy patrols made an occasional effort to move."[3]

The First Infantry Division made a three-year yearbook of 1967–1969. In that book this statement appears, "In July of 1969, the Big Red One received intensive resistance from the NVA."[58]

In a telephone conversation, Lt. Col. Vinson stated, "The one thing you are never going to be able to do is to tell of the pain many of us have suffered for all of these years. I don't think a week has gone by in the last twenty-six years that I haven't cried myself to sleep at least once thinking of this.[41]

Dec 30 at 1:00 p.m.

"There are two important lessons here: one, the infantry commander has command; tell your company what you want to do, but don't tell them how to do it. In other words, we were given an order to do a BDA and we did that BDA by aircraft. And when I was given the order to dismount the troops and use that particular company, that was wrong. That was a bad mistake. Lesson two: Don't let artillery run your AO (Area of Operation)."[4]

In a letter, Wully stated, "After talking to you and 2/6 I have finally found peace. I hope everyone that was there can finally achieve peace. I can now think of those days without the feeling of being eaten alive."[21]

Gilliam says, "You know, we was in so much, and we had to go in and pull the legs out all the time. Every firefight we was in and every battle is in the yearbook but that one. I went back and looked. We wasn't equipped to hit that mountain that day anyhow. We were a mechanized outfit."

In a telephone conversation, Hugh Evans, XO for Alpha stated, "I guess the lesson that I would like to see viewed by people that have the ability to make decisions [is], if you wouldn't send your own people on a mission, don't send anybody else to do it. If it doesn't make sense to sacrifice the lives of the soldiers under you for no apparent reason, then it makes no sense to sacrifice anyone else's life. There was nothing to be gained from the exercise. I see where Robert McNamara has recently said the same thing on a macro scale; there was nothing to be gained from the exercise after about 1967. There certainly was, in this particular case, no tactical advantage to the hill. It was not going to work."[44]

George Forrest commented, "I also have a problem coming under someone else's control. Every time it happened to me, even as a platoon leader or later as a company commander, it seemed that I got the worst jobs. The other people would rest their troops and work the people under them. There is a great deal of hue and cry right now about NATO and UN forces and not having US forces with the ability to operate independently of Allied Forces so people get used up."[34]

In a phone conversation, Jerry Campbell stated, "This is by far the dumbest thing I ever heard of. And to this day, I try to think that intelligent men would guide their fellow man through something like that. I've always told everyone that, and I don't talk about the war that much, but if I'm asked, this is what I say: 'The men that were sent over there with me, I would fight with them anywhere. They were hard-working men, and we just fought our butts off under very difficult conditions that we didn't control. America can be proud of the young men that they sent over to Vietnam. It's too bad that the soldier got a bad reputation. We never killed babies; we never did anything like that. We did what we had to and what we were told to do. We put our life on the line for our country and for our buddies. We were asked to do a lot, and if a lot of them have hurt in their hearts, hate in their hearts, I certainly understand it. We got a slap in the face for doing something that was more than we could do. I hope we have finally learned to fight a war to win it like we did in the Middle East.'"[33]

Dec 31 at 2:00 p.m. SFC Jack A. McCaffrey said, "At the time of this action I was assigned to the Enemy Order of Battle Section in First Division headquarters. There were two old special forces guys that wrote a book. I think they used one of the last names and the other one's first name. And they wrote a book; one of the stories that they wrote was about that—about that mountain, Nui Ba Den. They went down, these guys went down in there one time and they said the part they saw, before they got run out, was tunneled out. There was all kinds of ... one big cavern in there. In one place it was just full of supplies and tunnels running off just every direction. And they were so camouflaged so well from the outside you couldn't even see them. But they found the entrance by accident. It was real small ... Anyway, they got run out. They got down there a good distance before they were discovered."[42]

Bill interjected, "Our people had no idea what to expect on that mountain July 12, 1969." Jack continued, "That's just a failure of intelligence. Stuff hadn't been passed on. The army had people that had been looking around up there for years. We were up there in, I think it was January of '66 when the 2/2 was up there. They were a leg unit. The NVA had been there for a long time. They even were resupplied. A unit from 101st Airborne had a relay station on top of the mountain. They had a platoon that almost got overrun in '67. On July 12, they probably came up behind you and all around you."[42]

Chapter 20: Afterward

The men of the 2/2 (Mech) thought of themselves as members of a special unit. When we heard that Major General George Forsythe, Commanding General of the 1st Air Cavalry Division had told Major General Orwin C. Talbott of the 1st Infantry Division that while we were attached to the 1st Air Cavalry, he considered our Battalion the "Best Battalion in the theater," we were proud to hear it. In early June 1969 some changes took place in the leadership of the 2/2 (Mech). History reveals that the replacement commanders and staff were as competent as those that they replaced. The 2/2 (Mech) was well trained and continued to be well led.

The reconstruction of the battle fought by Alpha 2/2 (Mech),Charlie 2/2 (Mech) and supporting units on July 12-13, 1969 is from the accounts of the men that survived. The picture that emerges of Alpha 2/2 (Mech) is one of a trained, dedicated unit in an untenable situation. This writer gained an appreciation for the selfless performance of individuals fighting to reconstitute the team and care for each other. Valor, loyalty to each other, and loyalty to their unit were the order of the day.

The purpose of this book has been to tell their story. There has been no specific effort to assess blame. It must be acknowledged, however, that senior officers of the 25th Infantry Division interjected themselves into the chain of command of the 2/2 (Mech) at Battalion and at the Company level. These interjections served to cause violations of the nine classic principles of war.* Only valor, training and Standard Operating Procedures prevented Alpha 2/2 (Mech) from being defeated in detail.

On a lesser scale, it must be acknowledged that the previous portrayals of the battle, as told by the newspapers, were not accurate. Those who fought, particularly those who were killed in action, deserve to have their heroism, dedication to each other and dedication to their unit properly documented. More importantly, you have read about the real combat soldiers who served in the Vietnam War. You have read stories that many of these soldiers have never told anyone before. It is the case that these men were common men displaying uncommon valor.[58]

*The nine classic principles of war are: Objective, Offensive Action, Simplicity (Clearly expressed orders), Unity of Command, and Mass, Economy of Forces, Maneuver, Surprise and Security (Measures to prevent Surprise).

Chapter 21: Captain Dudley (Pete) Combs

I, Joe Ladensack, arrived at Fire Support Base Thunder IV in the early afternoon of May 22, 1969. Lt. Col. Michienzi said that he was very busy but that I would be assigned to Alpha Company. 1st Lt. Mike Mulhern, Alpha Company Mortar Platoon Leader, happened to be at Thunder IV, and he drove me to Quan Loi, where a brigade of the First Calvary was based. Alpha Company would be spending the night there.[7]

As we waited, suddenly Alpha Company roared up. The men and their tracks were covered with the red dust that permeated the area around An Loc. They had been busting jungle all day. My first thought was, *Is this an American unit?* They looked like they should be in a *Mad Max* movie. This first impression would drastically change in fewer than twenty-four hours.

Lt. Mulhern walked me over to Capt. Combs's APC and introduced me to Capt. Combs. After dismissing Mulhern, Combs abruptly said, "Sit down, Lieutenant." This began the most intense, enigmatic, impressionable relationship in my life until that time and since. Capt. Combs was only my commander for four weeks; nevertheless, his impact was profound!

Combs continued, "Do you recognize me?"

"No, sir," I stammered.

"You attended Infantry Officer Basic Course last year, didn't you? Well, I was the officer in charge of the map reading committee." Fear gripped every fiber of my body. I had a flashback to that part of my training.

Map reading was the hardest part of IOBC, and part of what had made it so hard was the captain who was constantly in everybody's face. "I'm going to Vietnam soon, and God help any lieutenant assigned to me who doesn't know how to read a map!" he boomed every day.

Continuing, Combs said, "Well, I hope you learned something because knowing where you are at all times is the most important skill in my company. You have ten days to show me that you can read a map, or I'll kick your ass out of Alpha and I don't care where it lands! I don't like lieutenants. Sergeants are better leaders than lieutenants. They know something. But the army says I have to have you—so here you are! Let me give you some advice. An infantry platoon is like a street gang. It will always have a leader, and it had better be you!!" I was then dismissed to Second Platoon, where 1st Lt. Dick Mailing was the platoon leader. He was about to be reassigned, and he was to teach me as much as possible in the next two or three days.

That night, Second Platoon was given the mission of setting up a mounted ambush about a klick away from the company. At one point, the entire platoon fell asleep. We were awakened by the screaming voice of Capt. Combs over the radio. After shouting obscenities for what seemed like an hour, he said, "Now that the NVA know where you are, I hope they kill all of you! I want both of you lieutenants to report to me first thing in the morning!" When we reported, Combs looked at Mailing and said, "I'm glad you are getting out of the company," and looking at me, he added, "For this little stunt, Second Platoon will pull point for the next ten days and the next ten night ambushes."

Suddenly, Michienzi's voice came over the radio and said that the recon platoon had been ambushed in the village of Minh Duc. Alpha was to reinforce them immediately. With Second Platoon pulling point, thus started thirty days of almost daily contact with the North Vietnamese 141st Regiment.

On June 25, 1969, Capt. Combs became the aide-de-camp for Maj. Gen. Orwin C. Talbott, the commanding general of the First Infantry

Division. Alpha Company had a new commander, Capt. Richard L. Buckles. Having pulled point and leg ambushes for ten days, my learning curve had been nearly vertical.[7]

In the fall of 1995, I was living with my wife and two stepsons in Sierra Vista, Arizona. When the telephone rang, I heard a voice from twenty-six years in the past. "Is this the Joe Ladensack who served with the 2/2 Mech in Vietnam in 1969? Well, this is Pete Combs. I'm going to a nephew's wedding in Phoenix and would like to stop by and visit you."

"Most certainly," I said. "Where are you now?"

"I'm five minutes from your house."

Pete knocked on the back door and said he had only a few minutes because he had to get to Phoenix for a rehearsal dinner. He stayed four hours. He accepted a glass of ice tea and said abruptly, "I have come to find out what makes you tick." He continued, "In combat you were so aggressive, not reckless. Why so? You see, I myself am a coward."

Surprised, I said, "Well, you certainly didn't seem that way to all of us in Alpha. Your men highly respected you. As a fact, all of your men said that if you had still been our Company Commander on July 12, things would have turned out much differently. First of all, the men, proud of the toughness of their CO, said you would have told that general to f--k off! Even if battalion insisted that we conduct the mission, you would have taken the APCs to the base of the mountain and sent only five or six men to do the BDA. When they found only big rocks, downed trees, and tunnels, you would have called them back and got the hell out of there! Your men respected you. In no way would you endanger their lives unnecessarily!"

Pete said, "We are getting off the point. Why were you so brave?"

I then told him that I had attended an all-boys prep school run by Jesuit priests. Every day, they hammered into us that, as individuals, we had a mission to complete here on earth. Our purpose was to find that mission and once we did, God would give us the means, grace, to complete it. "So," I said, "my motivation was religious. Besides, I've always been taught that the best defense is a good offense. My father was a firefighter for thirty years. He always said that the best way to save lives and property was to attack the fire as quickly and as aggressively as possible. To do this, you had to rely on your training, experience, and your gut instinct. You, Captain Combs, were the one to give me the training and experience."

Combs was surprised. He said, "How did I do that? I was your CO for only a month."

I then told him about what Major Forrest had told me when I first arrived in the battalion. "He said that Captain Kelly and you were excellent company commanders but taught your young lieutenants differently. I had learned that Kelly had wanted to be a friend with his officers and taught them with lectures and stories. You, however, threw us in the lake. His methods were verbal and visual. Your method was kinesthetic. That is the best way to me to learn. Those ten straight days of pulling point and ambushes were how I gained experience and learned to trust my gut."

"Well, what was it then that I taught you?"

I made a list for him:

1. Always look out for the welfare of your soldiers.
2. Be strict but fair in their discipline.
3. Never settle for mediocrity.
4. The maintenance of your vehicles is as important as training your men.
5. Know the enemy, and never assume that they can't do something.
6. Don't think those APCs with their .50-caliber machine guns make you invincible. If the enemy wants to destroy you, they will sacrifice enough men to do so.

7. Always have your infantry dig in at night. In a full-fledged night attack, it will be the M-60s on the ground that will save you.

8. Leave no doubt in your men's minds that you are the leader. Show it to them every day. Don't ask them to do anything that you haven't done already.

I continued, "You also taught me how to run a contact. I can remember the first contact I ran. You told all of the other platoons to stay off the net, and then you talked to me—and to me only. 'Okay, stud, you are going to be all right.' Your voice was very calm and steady. 'Calm yourself. Take deep and slow breaths. Look to your right and left. Make sure your men are on line and focused. Correct anyone by name who is off line or not paying attention. Tell your men to take their M-16s off safe. Tell them what you want them to do when the first shot is fired. Tell them if they see a bunker or an NVA they are free to fire without permission. Rush the bunker, grenade them, and move forward. The follow-on troops will search the bunkers. Keep your RTO behind you. Keep the tracks behind you. Move them up to gain fire superiority. Even after you overrun the bunkers, stay alert. A counterattack will surely come. Tell the medics to attend to the wounded.' That calm, deliberate walk-through helped me tremendously. It showed me that you cared for my well-being and that of my soldiers. I used that same method with my recon platoon. In the six months with the recon platoon, I didn't lose a single man and only had one slightly wounded. I was able to accomplish that because of you! You were the best teacher I ever had."

Astonished, Combs said, "I didn't know I did all that."

"I guess that was your gut instinct to do it that way. All of your teaching kicked into action on Nui Ba Den. Those who survived or had their wounds attended to can credit you."

We then had a lengthy discussion that I would characterize as one between a father in his seventies and a son in his fifties—both mature men with respect for one another, sharing what they have learned in life.[7]

A short time later, some of Alpha Company held a reunion in Harrison, Arkansas. Captain Combs attended that reunion and experienced the respect that he had earned so many years before. Dudley "Pete" Combs died a few months later from a massive stroke.

If I have rambled on, I apologize. What I have written is heartfelt and in some way shows the great admiration I have for this man and my thankfulness for serving with him. I am so thankful that we had that talk in Sierra Vista, Arizona, that day. It has been the grace that has helped me in the future missions presented to me.7

Chapter 22: Battle of Nui Ba Den—
Reflections of Joe Ladensack

In the past forty-six years, Alpha and Charlie Company have been telling stories about the battle they fought and the actions of the American and the NVA-Vietnam forces. The usual response has been 'How did any one of your survive?' After serious reflection I propose a plausible answer.[7]

American Actions

Simply stated, American actions were guided by bad decisions based on false assumptions after a review of faulty intelligence, leading to a complete military disaster. American senior commanders broke every one of the nine principles of war. They disregarded objective, simplicity, security, and most egregiously, unity of command. Only the actions of individual soldiers and the coordination of artillery and air support by 1st Lt. Mathews kept Alpha 2/2 (Mech) from being destroyed.

NVA/Viet Cong Actions

The commander of the NVA/Viet Cong forces had one simple mission— keep the Americans off the mountain and gather intelligence about enemy forces in the area from their superior observation point. To accomplish this mission, he had a rifle company with AK-47s, RPGs, and RPDs (light machine guns) with a detachment of snipers.

After having survived the B-52 strikes of the night before, he probably seriously considered the possibility of a full assault on his position. That assault would come from the base of the mountain and with an air assault from the top. His intelligence told him there was a battalion-sized force of armor and infantry in the area. Such an assault would begin with artillery and tactical air strikes, the standard American tactic.

In the early afternoon of July 12, 1969, no follow-up artillery or air strikes had taken place. Only a small infantry force approached the mountain. As they began to climb and approach his security zone, he allowed his soldiers to begin firing. *How stupid of those Americans to send such a small force*, he thought from his superior vantage point. The only problem had been a soldier prematurely firing an RPG out of nervousness.

As the Americans began to retreat, he concluded that their mission had been a BDA. However, the Americans had no cover. His unit was inflicting serious casualties upon the Americans. By SOP, his snipers were targeting radio operators and the officers and leaders who were always near them. He urged his men to increase their rate of fire until they had overwhelming fire superiority. This small unit no longer posed his position any threat. So he sent three- and four-men teams to scout the American flanks and rear. Their mission was to kill as many Americans as possible and warn him of any other approaching units. As the Americans continued to fall, he considered leaving his position and conducting an assault upon the now very small American unit. However, upon again considering his mission and the possibility that the Americans were setting a trap for him by getting him off the mountain and entering a kill zone, he decided against such an action. Furthermore, his recon teams had not returned (nor would they ever). The arrival of the APCs confirmed his assessment of the situation.

His soldiers continued to fire at the Americans as they retreated. He had completed his mission. He had his men take shelter in tunnels and behind boulders, anticipating artillery and air strikes. This is what the Americans always did. He thus protected his unit and eliminated any intelligence that the Americans might gain as to what those tunnels were and where they led.

The next day's attack by an armored force was also repulsed by fire superiority. The Americans then completely vacated the area. Mission complete!

Lessons Learned

Americans: "Where do we even start?"

NVA/Viet Cong: "Kill enough Americans and they will leave."[7]

His Woman Begs

When I heard they were building a Wall
Honoring the Vietnam War
It made me angry, I'd protested that war.
The policy of that war, the useless deaths.

So when I first came to the city of that Wall
I did not know you
I did not want to know you
And yet you were part of me.

But the Wall had a magnetic pull,
You had a magnetic pull
And visit after visit to that city
Time after time you pulled me back to the Wall

Each time I knew you more
You were my age, but you hadn't grown old.
At night in the dark, 58,000 voices spoke
And I heard your mother's crying.

Then I met him and he told me who you were
He told me how you had died.
Then he came with me to visit you.
He touched you and he cried.

I could feel his pain as you recognized him.
You called his name and he found you on the Wall.
He saw your face and he saw your smile.
He heard you die.

The magnetic pull tried to keep him there.
He didn't want to leave you,
Not then or now.
He wanted to save you, all of you or die with you.

He is not here today, I've come alone.
I've come to give thanks and to pray.
I've come to speak with you.

I've come to beg, beg you to let him go.
So, I find your names on the Wall.
I place a rose and tobacco beneath your names.

It made him angry when you died.
Did you know that he loved you?
You must know he can't forget you.

He cries in his sleep.
As I kneel here, I beg you to watch his back.
I pray to you to save him and I know you hear me.

I say to you, he needs you, help him he's dying.
He never forgives himself for living.
I beg you, help him to forgive himself.
You hear me say, I love him; I want him to live again.

You see this man stop beside me?
He has asked if I have someone on the Wall.
I say, "No, I love one of the walking dead."
He understands, he nods and walks on.

I know that you don't know me.
But you hear me, you are always listening.
They put you here to listen, you hear it all.
And you know you're not forgotten.

To all of you who know him and knew him to be good.
I know now what drew me here.
Only you can save him.
Only you can let him live.

—Diana Lee King (Wife of SP4 Danny King)[27]

Endnotes

1.   2/2 Radio Log for 2/2 (Mech) Bn of July, 12, 1968
2.   Twenty-Fifth Infantry Division After Action Report dated Nov. 24, 1969
3.   Twenty-Fifth Infantry Division Yearbook Dates Sept 1968–Sept 1969
4.   Lt. Col. Vinson's After Action Report for the dates June 9, 1969–Oct. 10, 1969
5.   First Infantry Division Yearbook II
6.   Alpha Company's Morning Report July 13, 1969
7.   2nd Lt. Joseph Ladensack (2/6) in a written statement dated May, 9, 1995, and many further conversations
8.   1st Lt. Mike Mulhern in a written report dated 1995
9.   Letter Franz Steidl sent to Marshall Prange HHC 2/2 (Mech) dated Feb. 25, 1993, and forwarded to Bill Sly
10.   Letter Franz Steidl sent to Bill Sly HHC 2/2 (Mech) dated Aug. 26, 1995
11.   Telephone conversations between Bill Sly and SP5 Elmer Dehaven (Doc D) that took place in early 1995
12.   Telephone conversations between Bill Sly and SP5 Mike Mirenda on Dec. 29, 1996
13.   Telephone conversations between Bill Sly and 1st Lt. Toney Mathews on Feb. 21, 1995.
14.   Two telephone conversations between Bill Sly and SP4 Ray Coursen (Hippie) on July 7, 1995, and SP4 Van Morrison (Van) on March 30, 1995
15.   Telephone conversations between Bill Sly and SP4 Ron Pilgrim
16.   Telephone conversations between Bill Sly and PFC Tennessee
17.   Telephone conversations between Bill Sly and PFC Robert Streightiff that took place March 25, 1995
18.   Telephone conversations between Bill Sly SP4 Lee Stember that took place Jan. 17, 1997
19.   Telephone conversations between Bill Sly and SP4 Chip Banks on March 23, 1995
20.   Telephone conversations between Bill Sly and S. Sgt. Philip Deering that took place on July 7, 1997
21.   Telephone conversations between Bill Sly and Sgt. Gary Wullenweber (Wully) that took place April 15, 1995

Appendix

The following are First Division Infantry orders, all approved in 1969 for Alpha Company soldiers who fought on July 12–13, 1969

- David Anderson: Gen Ord: 6918 PH
- Charles Banks: Gen Ord: 10941 BS, PH, ACM: Gen Ord: 10261
- Phillip Beck: Gen Ord: 6918 PH
- Jimmy Begay: Gen Ord: 13245 BS PH
- Mike Benefield: Gen Ord: 13246 BS
- Billy Bensen: *Capt. Driver:
- Joseph Bowers: Gen Ord: 13259 ACM PH
- Dennis Brown: Gen Ord: 10931 ACM PH
- Richard Buckles: KIA SS BS ACM 2nd OLC PH 1st OLC
- Jerry Campbell: Gen Ord: 13268: BS 2nd OLC
- Robert Childers: Gen Ord: 6918 PH
- Ronald Cohen: Gen Ord: 6918 PH
- Alberto Colon-Coto: Gen Ord: 13299 BS PH 1stOLC
- Leonard Compton: Gen Ord: 13260 ACM
- Ray Coursen: Gen Ord: 13262 BS 1st OLC
- Francisco Cruz: ACM PH
- Dominic Cuizio: Gen Ord: 9565 ACM 1st OLC PH 1st OLC
- Steven Cummins: KIA SS BS ACM PH 1st OLC
- Freddie Daniels: Gen Ord: 13258 ACM 1st OLC PH 1st OLC
- Robert Dayton: # Morning Report: PH
- Phillip Deering: Gen Ord: 13297 SS 1st OLC PH 1st OLC
- Elmer Dehaven: Gen Ord: 9908 SS
- Arthur Dibattista: Gen Ord: 13250 ACM
- Tennessee: Gen Ord: 6918 PH
- Richard England: KIA SS BS ACM PH

- Tim Frake: *
- Lawrence Frank: Gen Ord: 6918: ACM PH
- Chris Freeze: *Capt. Gunner
- Steven Friend: Gen Ord: 13256 ACM
- William Gillespie: Gen Ord: 13295 SS
- Maurice Gilliam: Given a PH# ACM 2nd OLC
- Bruce Gobio: Gen Ord: 15807 ACM
- Leonard Golden: *
- Charles Gunn: Gen Ord: 6918 PH
- James Hale: Gen Ord: 13261 BS
- Lawrence Horn: Gen Ord: 13255 ACM
- Bob Hall: Gen Ord: 13247 ACM PH 2nd OLC 6918
- Calvin Harris: KIA SS BS ACM PH
- Earl Herbert: Gen Ord: 13298 BS PH
- Cantor Hill: Gen Ord: 13296 SS PH 1st OLC
- Larry: Gen Ord: 13255 ACM Very Bad PTSD Do not contact him
- Alvin Howard: *
- Roger Hulsey: *
- Vernon Johnson: Gen Ord: 12964: SS 2nf OLC PH
- Dennis Jones: Gen Ord: 13266 BS
- Richard Karpinski: Gen Ord: 13267 BS
- Kevin Keleher: Gen Ord: 15667 BS 1st OLC PH
- George Kimmell: KIA SS BS ACM PH
- Daniel King: Gen Ord: 733 (issued 1970) BS 1st OLC
- Johnny King: KIA SS BS ACM PH
- Donovan Kolness: *
- Sammy Labastida: *
- Joseph Ladensack: Gen Ord: 9907 SS 1st OLC PH
- Dennis Lakins: Gen Ord: 13248 ACM
- Calvin Maguire: KIA SS BS ACM PH
- Toney Mathews: SS (1st Lt Mathews was the company FO)
- Bernard Matthews: *
- Fred Mathews: Gen Ord: 13272 BS 1st OLC
- Larry Miller: Gen Ord: 13301 BS
- Michael Miranda: *

- Kenneth: Gen Ord: 13251 ACM
- Van Morrison: Gen Ord: 8778 ACM
- Michael Mulhern: Gen Ord: 6964 PH
- James Nichols: Gen Ord: 13270 BS
- Robert Oerther: #
- Joseph Parez-Gonzales: #
- Donald Paxton: BS 2nd OLC
- Thomas Pedigo: Gen Ord: 13249 ACM 1st OLC
- Ron Pilgrim: Gen Ord: 13269 BS PH 2nd OLC #6916
- Bob Roberts: PH
- Charles Roberts: Gen Ord: 13484 PH
- John Rockafellow III: Gen Ord: 13252 ACM 1st OLC PH
- Ronald Rohden: Gen Ord 6922 PH
- Terry Shaw: Gen Ord: 13252 ACM PH
- Robert Sires: KIA SS BS ACM PH
- Clarance Smith: Gen Ord: 13254 ACM PH
- Lee Stember: ACM
- Charles Steward: Gen Ord: 13314 BS 3rd OLC PH
- Robert Streightiff: Gen Ord: 6918 PH
- Robert Tribble: Gen Ord: 13271 BS 1st OLC PH
- Daniel Wagnaar: KIA SS BS ACM PH
- Rickie Walker: Gen Ord: 6918 PH
- G Wallace: PH
- Donald Weber: *
- Don Wilkins: Gen Ord: 11615 BS
- Michael Williams III: Gen Ord: 13315 BS PH 1st OLC
- Gerald Wullenweber: Gen Ord: 8783 BS 2nd OLC

The following are First Infantry Division orders from July 12–13, 1969, that went to soldiers of Charlie Company 2/2(Mech) and were approved in 1969.

- Fred Baehr: Gen Ord: 12822: BS 1st OLC
- John Belvin: Gen Ord: 12729: SS PH
- Stephen Bergstrom: Gen Ord: 12368: ACM
- Steven Bradbury: KIA SS BS ACM PH

- James Brezovec: BS 2nd OLC 7-13
- Don Coughennower: Gen Ord: 12716: ACM
- Roger Dills: Gen Ord: 9861: ACM
- Donald Fisher: Gen Ord: 12821: BS 1st OLC
- Charles Geyer: Gen Ord: 12719: ACM
- James Gross: Gen Ord: 12718: ACM
- Kenneth Hillenbrand: Gen Ord: 12713 ACM 1st OLC
- Charles Horner: FO for C: BS
- Ralph Hoover: Gen Ord: 12853: ACM
- Carrol Howard: Gen Ord: 12709: BS
- Sergio Lugo: Gen Ord: 12721: BS
- Ralph Raitz: Gen Ord: 12710: ACM
- Larry Reeves: Gen Ord: 12827: ACM 14253: BS 2nd OLC
- Bob Roberts: PH
- Charles Roesel: Gen Ord: 12334: ACM
- Thomas Stillwell: Gen Ord: 12724: ACM
- Louis Stout: Gen Ord: 12830: ACM 1st OLC
- Larry Thorne: Gen Ord: 12826: BS
- Franklin Whaley JR: Gen Ord: 12830: ACM 1st OLC
- Robert Worrell: KIA SS BS ACM PH

The following are First Infantry Division Orders from July and August that went to soldiers of HHC 2/2 (Mech) and were approved in 1969.

- James Knox: Gen Ord: 13202: BS: 16410: SS: 14607: BS 1st OLC
- Jay McDevitt: Gen Ord: 12994: BS 3rd OLC
- William Sly: Gen Ord: 10040: BS*
- Newell Vinson: Gen Ord: 13175: BS

* No record of a Valor award found
# No record of Purple Heart found